BOWL to WIN

BOWL to WIN

DAVID BRYANT & TONY ALLCOCK
with EDWARD HORTON

In association with

An Imprint of HarperCollinsPublishers

ACKNOWLEDGMENTS

The publishers would like to thank the committee of the Falcon Park Bowling Club, Painswick, Gloucestershire for permitting photography on their premises, and to thank those members of the club who participated in the photographic sessions.

All photographs have been reproduced courtesy of Bowls International.

Artwork by WBP.

The publishers would like to thank the World Bowls Board for permission to reproduce their Laws of the game.

All rights reserved

First published in 1994 by
CollinsWillow
an imprint of HarperCollins*Publishers*
London

© Key Publishing Ltd 1994

The Authors assert the moral right to
be identified as the authors of this work

A CIP catalogue record for this book
is available from the British Library

ISBN 0 00 218523 7

Designed and produced by Brown Packaging Ltd

Printed and bound in Spain

CONTENTS

   Introduction   6

1 **The Mechanics of Bowling**   8
   Bowling equipment
   How to grip a bowl
   Stance and delivery

2 **Playing the Shots**   42
   Finding line
   Bowling to length
   The draw shot
   Running shots
   Firm woods
   The drive

3 **The Tactical Game**   68
   Greenspeed
   The wind factor
   The human factor
   Use of mat and jack
   Indoor and artificial outdoor surfaces
   Shot selection

4 **Singles, Pairs and Team Play**   110
   Singles
   Pairs
   The Team Game

5 **The Winning Formula**   134
   Mental approach
   Purposeful practice
   Sportsmanship

   Glossary   144
   Laws of the Game   148
   Index   160

INTRODUCTION

Our aim in the following pages is to provide the best possible instructional manual for our sport. We have both written extensively on the subject of bowls over the years, but not surprisingly our views are continually undergoing reappraisal in the light of experience. Of course the fundamentals of bowling technique and tactics reamain unchanged, but the emphasis on this element or that of bowls theory and its applicability to the aspiring bowler does change over time. And here you have our current thinking on every signficant aspect of the sport.

Starting with the selection of bowls and bowling equipment, we isolate the various elements of the game and give you our best joint advice. We do not, however, pretend for a moment that in either theory or practice we hold identical views. Ours has been a very successful partnership of equals, both personally and professionally, but neither of us has ever been tempted to subordinate his own individual style in the interests of uniformity. On most points of bowls theory we are in entire agreement, and at a tactical level we think as one, as much as that is possible given our different personalities. But in important matters of technique our styles are at some variance, to put it mildly, and where appropriate we explain why we as individuals play the way we do – and why we cannot in some instances recommend our techniques to others.

Whatever your level of proficiency – from the complete novice to the senior club performer, and beyond – you will, we believe, find much of value as well as interest here. We take you through the

INTRODUCTION

basic elements of grip, stance and delivery, and then describe as clearly as we can the various shots and their functions. Then, having given you our considered views on such critical matters as finding line and length, we turn to the all-important area of percentage play and shot selection. Clear diagrams illuminate the best examples we can think of to clarify your thinking as you approach a complicated head.

Both of us are experienced in every configuration of the game – at singles, in triples and fours, and of course at pairs, where we have been partners for the best part of a decade. There are significant differences between these versions of bowls, and we spell them out, along with the various roles demanded by the team game of each individual member.

Finally, there is the mental side of the game, and here we hope that our observations, made after many years of competitive play at the highest levels of the game will prove valuable to you as you step on the mat at a critical juncture in a game. Bowling should always be enjoyable, but the key to what we are trying to get across is perfectly expressed in the title – BOWL TO WIN!

Tony Allcock

David J Bryant

THE MECHANICS OF BOWLING 1

Mechanics may sound a dour way to begin a book on an exciting sport, but of course to perform any skill well you must have a sound grasp of fundamental technique. In the case of bowls the linchpin of good technique is a good delivery action – the means by which you send the bowl smoothly on its way to the target, time after time after time. And that comes down to grip, stance and delivery. But to begin at the very beginning, there is the matter of equipping yourself for the sport – essentially, choosing from amongst the bewildering array of bowls on the market.

THE MECHANICS OF BOWLING

BOWLING EQUIPMENT

If you are coming new to the game of bowls, the following information will repay careful reading. Right at the outset you must make an important purchase, and because the choice of bowls on the market today is so extensive you must equip yourself with knowledge in order to choose intelligently. If, on the other hand, you are already an active bowler, you might be advised to consider how well your bowls satisfy your bowling needs. Many bowlers of considerable experience and talent handicap themselves unwittingly by persisting with inappropriate woods.

The term wood is a charming anachronism, held over from the days when bowls were actually made of wood. The wood of choice was lignum vitae (literally, 'wood of life'), the densest of all hardwoods and an increasingly scarce resource in its native West Indies – because of its strength lignum was extensively used in aircraft production during the Second World War. It was not ecological awareness that caused lignum bowls to fall out of favour, however, but the practical advantages offered by modern technology in the form of the composition bowl. So while it is still possible to see old sets of lignum bowls in action – in fact many Crown Green bowlers actively seek them out – when you go shopping for a set of woods you will be offered a bewildering array of plastic bowls. All of these bowls will conform to regulation standards, which stipulate a minimum and maximum diameter and a maximum weight. The range is great enough to accommodate the normal range of hand size and individual physical strength.

Put at its simplest, the ideal bowl is the one that feels most comfortable resting in the hand and flows most smoothly from the hand onto the green during the bowling action. That said, bowling conditions are so variable and the distinctions manufacturers create between their products often so subtle that choosing bowls is not easy – for anyone. The authors may fairly be described as experts in the matter, and yet they too can find themselves torn between the conflicting claims of one

Just a sample of the range of bowls and bowling equipment devised for the modern game, to suit all surfaces and all weathers.

bowl and another, one size and another, one weight and another. The best guidance they can offer – and in the course of their coaching there is no subject upon which their help is more keenly sought – is that you begin not in the sports equipment shop but in the company of experienced bowlers. Ask them to explain their choice to you, and the pros and cons of the various bowls they have used. Try to sort out the relationship between size and weight, and handle as many types of bowl as you can. If you encounter a charitable bowler (not a difficult task!) ask if you can borrow a set for a trial.

Things to consider

While personal 'feel' is the ultimate arbiter, these are the objective factors:

SIZE: There are advantages to big bowls (they tend to run truer), so the general rule is to choose the largest you can handle comfortably. But do not 'stretch' yourself to do so. A bowl that is even slightly too big will create tension in the hand, and that will more than negate any marginal advantage provided by size. One way of assessing optimum size is to encircle the bowl with thumbs and middle fingers. A bowl that fits snugly but comfortably within that circle is about right. If you have to stretch to make the fingers join, it is too big. If the fingers overlap, it is unnecessarily small. Another test is to hold the bowl with your fingers spread naturally and turn your hand over. If you can hold the bowl like that without fear of dropping it then it is not too big.

WEIGHT: One of the advantages of the composition bowl is that it can be (and is) heavier for its size than a lignum bowl. Weight of bowl is a complicated subject because it cannot be viewed in isolation from bowling conditions, but all things being equal (which they rarely are) there

These lurid bowls were prototypes for possible use during televised indoor tournaments – to add more than a dash of colour! In fact, black and mahogany remain the only authorised colours for tournament use.

THE MECHANICS OF BOWLING

The largest bowl you can comfortably handle – without stretching – is the best size to go for. One way of checking is to see if you can hold it easily with your hand turned over – if so, it is not too big. Women, with their generally smaller hands, usually tend to prefer a heavy bowl for the size.

BOWL TO WIN

BOWLS WEIGHTS AND SIZES

The World Bowls Board gives the following indication of the range of bowl sizes:

Size in inches	Size number	Actual metric (mm)	Rounded off metric (mm)
4 5/8	0	117.4	117
4 3/4	1	120.7	121
4 13/16	2	22.2	122
4 7/8	3	23.8	124
4 15/16	4	125.4	125
5	5	127	127
5 1/16	6	128.6	129
5 1/8	7	130.2	130

THE REGULATIONS STATE:

Bowls made of wood (lignum vitae) shall have a maximum diameter of 5 1/4 inches (134mm) and a minimum diameter of 4 9/16 inches (116mm) and the weight shall not exceed 3lb 8oz (1.59kg). Loading of bowls made of wood is strictly prohibited.

For all International and Commonwealth Games matches, a bowl made of rubber or composition shall have a maximum diameter of 5 1/8 inches (131mm) and a minimum diameter of 4 9/16 inches (116mm) and the weight shall not exceed 3lb 8oz (1.59kg).

Every bowl used in competition must be tested to make sure that it conforms to the minimum bias.

THE MECHANICS OF BOWLING

is one point always in favour of the heavier bowl. Following a collision between two bowls of different weight the lighter bowl will travel further than the heavier bowl. This gives the heavier bowl more stability in the head, an obvious benefit.

The response by bowls manufacturers has been to make bowls in two weights: medium and heavy. The heavy bowl can weigh as much as a medium bowl two sizes larger, and it is much favoured by bowlers with small hands (most women opt for them). Those who are able to handle the larger sizes are likely to find medium weight sufficient, especially for outdoor conditions where damp greens can sink beneath the pressure of a really heavyweight bowl.

BIAS: The characteristic arc described by a bowl results from its centre of gravity being slightly off-centre (its bias). Every bowl manufactured is tested against the World Bowls Board's Master Bowl, to ensure that it complies with the minimum stipulated bias. Beyond that, there is no limit to the legal bias, so bowls come in a variety of biases to suit individual preferences and bowling conditions experienced. At the extremes are water-logged, sluggish British greens which largely negate bias, and the lightning-quick greens characteristic of the

The composition bowl began to supplant lignum vitae during the 1950s and 60s, and is manufactured to rigorous standards. Many bowlers display lifelong loyalty to a favourite set of 'woods'.

BOWL TO WIN

Southern Hemisphere which greatly accentuate it. For the former, the heavily-biased or bending bowl is preferable, for the latter, the straighter-running bowl is almost essential.

It is easy enough for the average British bowler to ignore the demands of Australian conditions, but the situation has become complicated by the great and growing popularity of indoor bowling. Indoor carpets lie somewhere between the two extremes, certainly much quicker than outdoor British greens under all but the most ideal circumstances. Manufacturers now promote special indoor models, although whether they form a separate category of bowls (rather than being described simply as straightish bowls) is debatable. Certainly, it is the distinction between straightish and wide-swinging bowls that you must make, and here again you should try out as many bowls as you can before committing to a purchase.

Some players are snobbish about the minimum-bias bowl, on the grounds that cutting down the arc reduces the level of skill (or even the aesthetic appeal of the game). Ignore this completely. If you can bowl better with a straight-running bowl use it, although you will find that it has its disadvantages. There is a trade-off between the superior accuracy of the straight-running bowl and its more limited ability to curl around intervening bowls. Conversely, a really wide-swinging bowl can go where others cannot, but it is more difficult to control accurately. Generally speaking, for all-purpose British bowling, outdoors and indoors, you will not go far wrong with a medium-bias bowl. This is the personal choice of the authors and of most top British bowlers.

GRIPS: The old lignum woods (which both authors used in their earliest days) were smooth all over, but with the introduction of composition bowls, grips became an option. So they remain: some bowlers, including David Bryant, feel these dimples encircling the bowl interfere with comfortable handling and rarely use them (they can be attached and detached at will); others, including Tony Allcock, find them invaluable, especially under cold or wet conditions

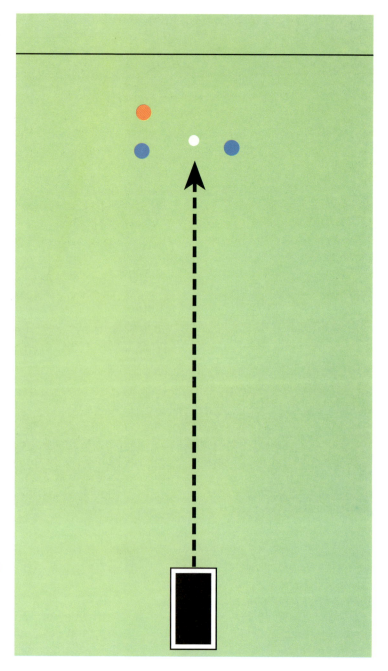

Heavy conditions and extreme pace can effectively neutralise bias – so the drive shot is played directly on target.

THE MECHANICS OF BOWLING

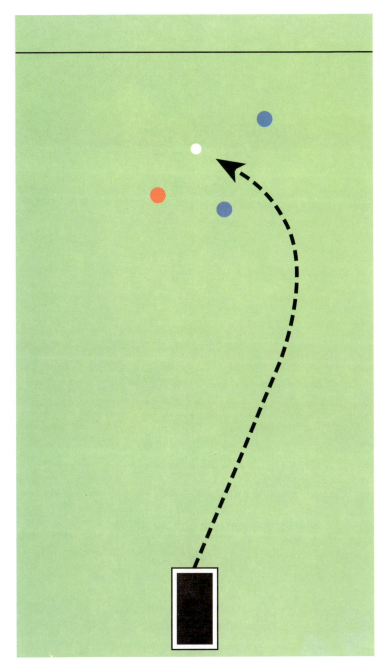

On really fast greens (such as are found in the Southern Hemisphere), the natural bias of the bowl is exaggerated. In such conditions, the straighter running bowl is preferred (to keep the arc within manageable proportions), whereas in heavy British conditions, the more heavily-biased bowl finds favour.

where they want a little more than a naked bowl to hang onto. You will work that one out for yourself.

If you happen to prefer mahogany to black, or vice versa, indulge yourself. Similarly, bowls may come with or without insignia, monograms, or whatever else you have in mind.

15

BRYANT'S CHOICE

'In the course of my long career I have used a vast array of bowls, beginning with lignum. Although it is a little narrow across the palm, my hand is reasonably large and I have always felt comfortable with Size 6. That is a big bowl, and the medium weight is heavy enough for me. If I have a favourite bowl it is the Australian-made Henselite Supergrip. I enjoyed great success with a set of these during the 1970s, but decided to put them up for a charity auction. Then I had to borrow one back and get Henselite to make me another set modelled on the original, so much did I miss it!

'Having said that, I am not committed to a single set of bowls. Bowling conditions are too varied for that. There are two other Henselite bowls that form part of my regular armoury, the Classic II and the Indoor Henselite. The Classic II is a tighter-running bowl than the Supergrip, and it is really designed for the Southern Hemisphere. However, I find it just about right for the indoor game. The Indoor describes itself, being specifically designed for carpet-play, although as you will see I put no importance on that term 'indoor'. To me, anything described as 'indoor' is just a tightish-running bowl with characteristics that make it suitable for particular conditions (wherever those conditions are found).

'During the 1988 World Championships (outdoors) in New Zealand, where the greens were running exceptionally fast, I decided that my normal Henselites would swing far too much, so I lighted on the Indoor Henselite as being a practical alternative, even though I had never bowled with them before. Henselite bowls have always been known as late swingers, where the

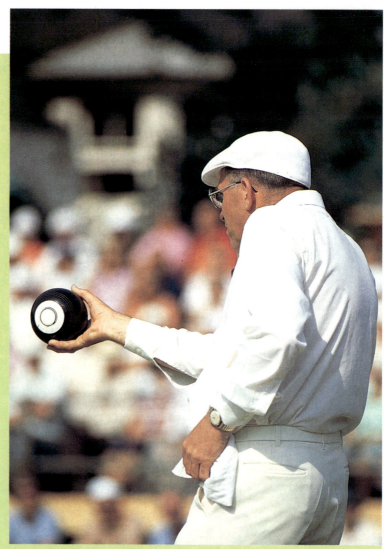

arc described is something like a hockey stick. But the Indoor Henselite is very different from its stablemates, in that it describes more of a banana arc, almost uniform from start to finish. In fact these bowls were absolutely perfect for the conditions, and I won the singles title without losing a game.

'Finally, so much do I believe in using the biggest bowl possible that I am now experimenting indoors with Classic IIs size 7! This runs completely counter to normal practice, which is to move down in size with increasing years, but there it is. In fact, you will likely find that you can move up or down one size from your optimum, so do not be surprised if you decide to ring the changes.'

ALLCOCK'S CHOICE

'Like David I use Henselite bowls – but there all similarity ends! My hand is slightly smaller than his so I have always used a size 5, and to get the weight up (which I think important) I go for the heavy bowl. That difference between us is purely in response to physical difference, but thereafter it is a matter of our different psychologies.

'I well understand David's case for selecting bowls to suit the conditions. But to me that has always been outweighed by the fact that it complicates your bowling. When I am under the pressure of competition I have quite enough on my mind without concerning myself about the particular bowl in my hand – about whatever may distinguish it from yesterday's bowl. In particular, if I am bowling badly, the last thing I want is doubt creeping into my mind about my selection of bowls (and remember, unlike the tennis player who may swap rackets a dozen times in the course of a match, you must stick with the bowls you have chosen).

'I have therefore persisted with my tried and tested woods for a decade. In all that time I have never been tempted to be unfaithful to them – until now! I am finally having to come to terms with the current conditions of outdoor bowling in England. **The greens have become so heavy (a combination of excessive rainfall and indifferent green-keeping) that I have decided to start out in the spring with a medium-weight bowl and one a size smaller as well.** In stepping up a size at his age David is clearly the exception to nature's rule, but I find it increasingly difficult to cope with size 5 in the cold and wet. I spend so much time drying every last particle of moisture from the bowl, polishing and polishing, that I am in danger of losing my concentration.

'So it is that I am going against my conviction by attempting to suit bowls to conditions. As (if) fine weather and good greens appear, I'll return to my old friends, and of course I will continue to use them indoors and in the Southern Hemisphere. This is a huge wrench for me, the result of much soul-searching, and in case you think that I have come around to David's point of view after all this time, the following tale will put the matter in perspective.

'David describes how he won the World Championship in New Zealand using Indoor Henselites. What he does not relate is what happened to those bowls. A friend of my brother's, Ken Oliver, showed David and me great kindness and hospitality during our stay in New Zealand. At the end of our stay, David calmly gave him the winning bowls! An act of great generosity, of course, but to me, from my perspective, with my attachment to my bowls, utterly unthinkable.'

BOWL TO WIN

Legendary athlete Steve Ovett's nephew, Oliver, bowls in regulation dress – from white shirt down to those mandatory brown shoes.

Clothing and equipment

The authors hold strong views on this subject, although for a reader who has no experience of bowling in this country, these views might appear to be rudimentary common sense, hardly worth expressing. There are two important issues here, one concerning money, and how bowlers feel about spending it, the other about the social attitudes of the bowling establishment.

Compared with equivalent sports, bowling is a great bargain. A set of first-rate bowls (which will last indefinitely) hardly costs more than a good tennis racket, and a fraction of what top-flight golf clubs would set you back. Club fees are modest, and would turn a committed tennis player green with envy. Golfers pay the earth to enjoy the facilities of a good club. The irony here is that because bowlers are able to enjoy their game on the cheap, they are inclined to view any additional expense as an imposition. So it is when it comes to the matter of buying clothing, with footwear being the most important single item. Too often bowlers skimp on bowling shoes, assuming that a cheap pair will be just as serviceable as an expensive pair. They will not. Uncomfortable, badly constructed shoes will bring you misery, and you should be prepared to lay out proper money for a decent pair.

Similarly with weatherproof gear – a must for bowling outdoors in our climate. Golfers and others who deliberately set out walking for any distance in wet weather routinely wear waterproof anoracks that have

THE MECHANICS OF BOWLING

a special vapour-permeable lining. What this 'breathable' lining does is allow perspiration to escape into the atmosphere, rather than condense inside the clothing. If you were to show their owners conventional bowler's waterproofs they would express sympathy, if polite, laugh outright if not. So golfers stride drily down the fairway – while bowlers slowly poach themselves in the drizzle. Of course bowls waterproofs are much cheaper, but it would be a red-letter day for our sport if there were sufficient demand for the better type to justify their manufacture.

Turning from the clothing itself, there is the vexed issue of official attitudes to what constitutes proper apparel on the green. White trousers and shirts for the men, similar skirts and blouses for the women are an attractive feature of the game, as they are for cricket. But in this country these handsome outfits are marred by shoes of regulation brown.

Bowlers in Britain are now permitted to complement their white clothes with smart white shoes (as worn here by Scotland's Willie Wood).

BOWL TO WIN

Why? Why not matching white shoes, which we wear bowling indoors? The only half-reasonable answer put forward is that if someone were standing behind the jack in white shoes it might impair the bowler's vision. It says a lot for eyesight down under that our antipodean friends have never experienced this drawback to white shoes!

The niggle about white shoes is as nothing compared to the clothing restrictions imposed on women bowlers – always assuming that a club is enlightened enough to allow them in as

Weatherproof gear is an essential, especially for bowling outdoors in the unpredictable British climate. A sudden downpour brings proceedings to an abrupt, often amusing halt, but a steady drizzle can easily bring misery to an ill-prepared bowler.

ALLCOCK'S RECOLLECTION: BLIND AUTHORITY

As patron of the English National Association of Visually Handicapped Bowlers, I was delighted to learn that the partially-sighted Somerset bowler Ann Bryant (no relation) had won her opening match in the 1993 county championships. This was not a special tournament for handicapped bowlers but the regular county championships – so this was an achievement anyone would cheer, you might think! She had won her match with no assistance whatever, except in the trivial matter of asking her opponent to check that her jacks were centred. No problem – at least so we all thought.

'Later on that evening, Ann received a telephone call from a tournament official informing her that she could not take further part in the tournament because she was unable to set the jack unaided. Even if you love the sport as much as I do it is hard not to despair of it when you come up against such an example of boneheaded officialdom.

THE MECHANICS OF BOWLING

members, rather than just to make the tea and sandwiches. They must wear skirts with a specified pleat, a specified length below the knee, and top it all with a white hat of specified design. Little wonder that many women who become attracted to the sport through television coverage recoil from taking it up when they discover this reality. They simply refuse to kowtow to such fustiness, and who can blame them? Television has done much to popularise bowls, not least by dispelling its middle-class and middle-aged image. So far, so good. But outmoded dress codes and blatant sexual discrimination are no way to appeal to the younger generation, and what sport can afford to spurn the young?

Women bowlers (right) are much more heavily circumscribed in their choice of apparel than men. The same white clothing and brown shoes are mandatory, but the dress regulations extend to the skirt length and even the pleat. As for the hat design, its attractiveness may be a matter of opinion, but wearing it is not a matter of choice. Such strict dress regulations can hardly appeal to the young (above) – and it is they who are the lifeblood, and future, of the game.

HOW TO GRIP A BOWL

As is the case with so much of the bowling action, sensible advice about how you hold the bowl in preparation for delivering it must begin with your own instinctive 'feel' for it. If you were to pick up a bowl for the very first time and hold it comfortably in your hand, fingers spread naturally to secure it without throttling it, that would provide a strong clue to the type of grip most suitable for you.

There are basically two ways to grip a bowl: either you rest it easily in the palm of your hand with the thumb more or less acting as a passenger, or you hold it further forward in the fingers, with the thumb coming towards the top of the bowl and playing an active part in the activity. There are a couple of variations worth mentioning, but in essence that is the choice – the cradle grip or the claw. Both have their attractions.

Cradle

The cradle grip is bound to feel comfortable, for it is barely a grip at all. The bowl simply rests in the palm. Not only is the thumb resting idly, the fingers are simply cupping the bowl, not gripping it. A supremely lazy grip, then, but its attractions are not to be underestimated. For one thing, its utter simplicity means that the cradle grip can hardly go wrong, in the technical sense. Because it requires so little muscular co-ordination between the various parts of the hand, it will not be prone to the sort of inconsistency that can always plague more complex movements.

The cradle grip has a considerable following in Britain (especially in Scotland) because the complete freedom of release gives maximum power for minimum effort. If you have bowled on a

For the cradle grip the bowl rests comfortably in the palm, fingers and thumb cupping rather than gripping it. The cradle provides maximum power for minimum effort (useful on heavy greens) with minimal control for touch shots (a liability on fast greens).

THE MECHANICS OF BOWLING

soggy green you will appreciate the benefit of that. By the same token it can compensate for physical weakness or for a small hand, because it is possible to use a larger bowl with the cradle grip.

The flip side of these virtues are predictable vices. Freedom of delivery can easily degenerate into loss of control, which means the bowl will wobble off on its journey, or in the worst case be embarrassingly lost altogether. In wet conditions this grip can be almost impossible to control; on very fast surfaces, palming the bowl away in such a freewheeling manner would seem to guarantee the very antithesis of the fingertip control demanded. The cradle grip has few devotees in the Southern Hemisphere.

There is a compromise version of the cradle, which goes some way to removing its drawbacks while maintaining its essential virtues. In this grip the bowl still rests in a relaxed palm, cradled by the fingers. But this time the thumb comes up the side of the bowl perhaps as far as the centre of the disc, which brings it into play in a guiding role. The advantage to using the thumb, even in a supporting role, is that it provides a more solid hold on the bowl without locking it in an iron-like vice.

The modified cradle represents a compromise between the virtues and vices of the true cradle. The thumb comes up the side of the bowl, perhaps as far as the centre disc, giving a more secure hold without constricting the bowl in a true grip. While in heavy conditions Tony Allcock uses the true cradle grip, he is pictured here using the modified cradle.

BOWL TO WIN

Claw

The claw grip really is a grip. The bowl is held mainly by the fingers and thumb. There is little or no contact with the palm of the hand, most of the weight being taken on the middle finger which forms the extension of the arm at the point of delivery. The running surface of the bowl is placed squarely on the middle and third fingers – the first finger helps, but the little finger is of little use and become a nuisance if it strays up the side of the bowl. The thumb comes up the side of the bowl to rest on or near the large ring.

The claw is the most widely used of grips. It obviously provides more sensitive control than the cradle, and its advocates claim that they can adjust the weight of the shot simply by varying the finger and thumb pressure on the bowl. If there is one grip that can claim to be all purpose, suitable for all conditions, it is the claw.

Its only real drawback is the **danger of over-gripping.** Beginners especially are in danger of clutching the bowl in a death-grip, as though reluctant to let it go. This makes for a strangulated delivery, and the bowl will wobble on delivery. This will be seen at its worst when the bowler is using woods that are on the small side.

The finger grip

On the quick surfaces of the Southern Hemisphere there is widespread use of an extreme version of the claw, called the finger grip. Here, the bowl comes even further forward in the fingers, with the thumb coming right to the top of the bowl. The finger grip provides maximum sensitivity for those very delicate shots demanded by the quickest greens, while the high thumb position tends to cut down on the bias, again especially useful when driving on fast greens. This grip is not suited to the conditions normally encountered in outdoor British bowling.

Whatever the grip, it must feel comfortable and tension free, with the fingers extended parallel to the running surface of the bowl. The bowl will then leave your hand straight as your palm extends outward in the direction of your

David Bryant uses the claw grip under all circumstances.

THE MECHANICS OF BOWLING

For the claw grip the bowl rests mainly in the fingers, having little contact with the palm. The thumb comes far up the side of the bowl to provide a really secure hold. Most bowlers favour some form of claw grip.

The finger grip is an extreme version of the claw. The bowl comes further foward in the fingers and the thumb moves to the top of the bowl. This grip provides maximum sensitivity and control (with minimal power), and it is popular in the Southern Hemisphere.

bowling line. If you allow the fingers to stray across the line of intended delivery you may scoop or bump the bowl onto the surface, and it will get off to a wobbly start. The likelihood is that the bowl will not leave the hand on the intended line, and even if by some chance it does, a bowl not launched on an even keel will have deviated from the intended line by the end of its run – just what you are aiming *not* to do when you launch a bowl on its run towards the head!

STANCE AND DELIVERY

From a technical standpoint, the only thing that matters in bowls is that you must be able consistently to deliver a bowl along a chosen line with predictable weight. Now, it would appear obvious that to achieve this goal the ideal delivery should be a flowing movement executed with fine skill from a perfect stance with absolute economy of motion. At the other extreme, a contorted flailing of arms or legs which leaves the bowler nearly prostrate on the green would seem to guarantee failure. In reality, this is not necessarily the case. Allowing for a little exaggeration in the above contrast, the deliveries could achieve a similar success rate. The crucial factor is how a bowl leaves your hand (how it is 'grassed'), not what goes on before. Providing a delivery follows a consistent pattern and the grounding of the bowl is sweet – once lyrically described as the process of 'decanting' the bowl onto the surface – then your bowl should follow its intended line.

The stance provides balance

The reason for developing a good bowling technique is entirely to do with consistency. Viewing the stance in isolation, you will never achieve consistent results if you keep varying the stance, because if you do so you are hopelessly complicating the rest of the equation that all must add up to a consistent delivery, shot after shot, day after day. It follows, therefore, that the stance must become second nature, and if it is to be that, above all it must provide you with proper balance. View the stance as the platform for your delivery. The delivery itself should be a natural extension of the stance – the stance in motion.

Both authors have extensive coaching as well as playing experience, and from both they have concluded that it is folly to try to impose any particular delivery style on other bowlers. Long before he or she ever picks up a bowl, the novice, even the young novice, has acquired physical traits that govern locomotion – movement in all its multiplicity of forms. These are so ingrained as to be

The main reason for developing a smooth, flowing delivery is that it provides the surest way of 'grassing' the bowl in a consistent manner.

THE MECHANICS OF BOWLING

instinctive, and it is better to work with this natural material than to kick against it. However you feel most natural grounding a bowl should be taken as the starting point for developing a successful technique. The only absolute constraint upon the action is that at the moment of delivery, when the bowl leaves the hand and touches the surface of play, at least one foot must be on or over the mat. If not, it is a foot fault.

It is often said that no two bowlers ever employ exactly the same delivery, and given the infinite variety of physical peculiarities of the human race this may be strictly true. Nevertheless, for practical purposes there are only a few plausible methods of setting a bowl in motion, and you will rarely see a bowler whose delivery does not conform, however badly it may be executed, to one of those described below.

BOWL TO WIN

Athletic

Some version of the athletic stance, also called the upright, is by far the most commonly used. This is especially true for bowlers who started young, because it is the natural way of rolling a ball. Give toddlers an orange, and if they decide to roll it they will simply bend their knees and send it across the floor. The athletic stance is no more than that instinctive action.

Stand comfortably on the mat, feet in line with the shot and bodyweight evenly distributed. Hold the bowl around the level of the diaphragm, or higher if it feels more comfortable. Bend your knees as you swing the bowl backwards, step smoothly forward with the leg opposite the bowling arm, planting the foot in line, and release the bowl. In the extreme version of the athletic stance the back is ramrod straight, but there is nothing to be gained by a parade-ground bearing. The chief merit of the athletic stance is that it is completely natural and supremely comfortable (for those who are fit). It is equally suited to all shots from the most delicate to the most powerful – and for the latter it is really essential, for in no other way can you get the entire momentum of your body behind the shot. If you find the athletic stance to your liking, look no further.

There is an an exaggerated form of the athletic delivery which is sometimes given a distinct name, the Scottish Runner. In it the bowler puts so much body weight over the bowl that his follow through propels him off the mat and up the green. The great Scottish player Willie Wood fairly charges after his bowl! It is a way of responding to the problems posed by the heaviest greens, to be found in Scotland, when every ounce of force must be put behind the shot.

The English and Scottish international Hugh Duff (right) follows through from the athletic stance, while Scotland's Willie Wood surges up the rink as he puts his entire bodyweight over the bowl – the classic Scottish Runner.

THE MECHANICS OF BOWLING

Crouch

For millions of television viewers the crouch stance is synonymous with David Bryant. The degree of the crouch can vary, but in the full Bryant crouch the legs are fully bent with the entire body weight being taken by the backs of the legs. If you try that and are less than fully fit you may well find it uncomfortable, to put it mildly. In addition, the way Bryant keeps his feet so close together on the mat when he takes up his stance would give many people anxieties about their balance. More commonly, the crouch stance begins with the feet placed rather more apart and with the left foot (for right-handers) in a forward position off the mat.

Whatever the particular crouch, the bowler must rise from it to the athletic stance in order to make the delivery – you could never generate sufficient power if you remained in the crouch. Whether the bowler comes partially or fully into the upright position during the delivery will often depend on the pace of the green and the weight of shot required, rising higher for greater weight. Two claims are made for the crouch stance. Because your eye is close to ground level it may help you sight the line better, as witness the way snooker players get right down over the cueball. Secondly, coming up into the athletic stance in that way cuts down on the movement involved through the swing, and this may result in increased control.

The inimitable David Bryant crouch, with all bodyweight supported by the legs. Once Bryant has settled on his line (the reason he favours the crouch) he rises to the height demanded by the weight of shot and then delivers, as though from a modified athletic stance.

BOWL TO WIN

The powerful Australian, Rob Parrella, prepares to drive from the semi-crouch or low-athletic stance. More bowlers use a version of this stance than any other.

Semi crouch or low athletic

The confusing nomenclature fairly reflects the 'in-betweenness' of this stance. It is easier to describe it as a variant of the athletic rather than the crouch. If from the athletic stance you begin to incline your body forward and bend your knees, you are departing from it – in the direction of the crouch. You may find it comfortable to bend the knees more than the back, or vice versa. Within reason, anything goes. When it was stated earlier that the athletic stance, in some manner or other, is the most widely used among bowlers, it is in this modified version that you will usually see it.

Except when a full-blooded drive is called for, this compromise stance has all the merits of the true athletic, with the advantage that you are nearer the ground, therefore cutting down on the totality of the movement and minimising the chance for error. But it does have a potential drawback. In the true athletic or true crouch stance you can be pretty sure that you are doing it the same way every time – in either case there are plenty of points of reference. But how far in-between is your particular version of it? And is it the same today as it was yesterday – or as it was the previous shot? Always remember that achieving consistency is the secret of a successful delivery.

THE MECHANICS OF BOWLING

Fixed

However radically different they may look, all athletic and crouch stances have more in common than separating them. This is because, whatever the starting point, at the critical point of delivery they are enabling the bowler to do the same thing, which is to stride forward along the line while swinging the bowling arm through to the point of release. This combination of forward body movement and arm movement allows the bowler maximum controlled power without necessitating an exaggerated backswing. Take away the forward body movement and you greatly increase the demands on the arm. This is the principal characteristic of the fixed stance.

The fixed stance requires the bowler to take up position on the mat with the left foot (for a right-hander) planted firmly down the line of delivery. In a true fixed stance the leading foot has completed the full step, which does away with secondary leg and body movement altogether. The free hand grasps the knee or thigh of the leading leg to provide stability. It is of critical importance that the bowler feels balanced in this position, and the best way to achieve that is to start from the athletic stance, step down the line of delivery and then settle comfortably over the leading leg, which supports most of the body weight. The bowl can be rested on the ground beside the leading foot.

There are pros and cons to any stance, and while the authors would never recommend a fixed stance to a normally fit player, it does have its strong points. Because the body is in a position where the only moving part during the delivery is the arm, all potential difficulties involved in co-ordinating hand and eye, step and body dip are automatically avoided. There is plenty of time to check line and assess length, and to focus completely on that single movement of the arm.

Against that, it must be said that the fixed stance has a serious drawback. Because the step has already been taken you lose the momentum provided naturally by the forward movement of the body. This places the entire burden of the shot on the arm and shoulder. This is a severe limitation on all but the very fastest greens, and even there if you want to play a genuine power shot. To play with anything like driving weight on a heavy green puts the backswing under intolerable strain. Moreover, the follow through is curtailed. So it is that the fixed stance is usually only employed by those whose physical condition requires it – the stiff of limb, back-pain victims, sometimes the overweight.

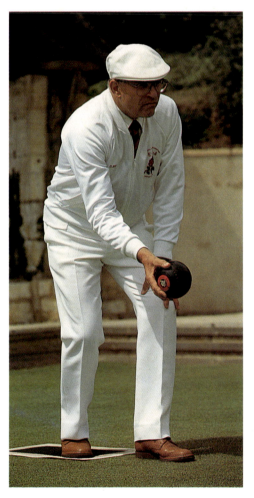

David Bryant demonstrates a fixed stance, which he never employs himself because of its obvious restrictions. All momentum must be generated by arm and shoulder alone, so this stance is really only appropriate for those whose physical limitations make it a necessity.

BOWL TO WIN

South African Clinic

Also called the semi-fixed stance, the South African Clinic is so named because it was developed to a high level in that country by the influential bowls theoretician Dr Julius Serge.

The key to this delivery is the positioning of the back foot and its weight-bearing function prior to delivery. To achieve it, stand on the mat facing the line of delivery with your weight on the back foot. Then take a short step forward with the front foot, making sure to keep your weight on the back foot – this is vital to Serge's theory. The body may be upright or inclined towards the line, the free hand resting on the knee or supporting the bowl, just so long as the weight remains firmly on that back foot. Now step forward again and deliver as though from the athletic stance, with the natural transference of weight.

This is not as awkward or contrived as it sounds, and there are many fine bowlers in South Africa and elsewhere who achieve excellent results with this stance. It allows for a much freer delivery action than the true fixed stance (although, from its place of origin it will be clear that it was not developed with heavy greens in mind), and of course it shares the advantage of having the line mapped out in advance. That and the fact that the weight is kept on the back foot for as long as possible is claimed to 'fix' the bowl on the chosen line with more certainty than any other type of delivery. Whether that theoretical benefit outweighs the practical drawback in relation to smoothly-delivered power is open to question.

Two views of the South African Bill Moseley, employing the South African Clinic or semi-fixed stance. It combines great stability with much more freedom of movement than the fixed stance.

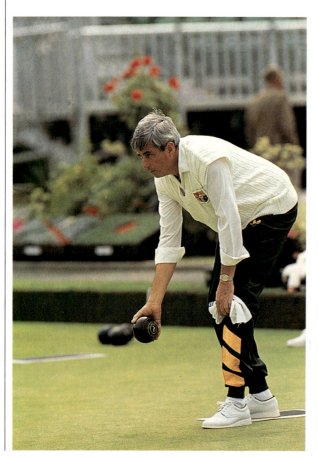

THE MECHANICS OF BOWLING

Swing and follow through

Whatever stance is adopted, it is only a means to an end. The delivery of the bowl is what matters, and while in practice the entire action is a single activity, it is important to look at the arm movement in isolation. If that goes awry it will spoil an otherwise textbook action. If it is right, it will compensate for any eccentricity in the rest of the action, which is, after all, no more than a technique for ensuring success at this final point.

The arm action is a pendulum swing – first one way, then the other. Assuming the athletic stance, the bowl is swung back passing the body while the front foot moves forward in a natural walking step along the line of delivery. The strength of the delivery will be governed by the length of the backswing. The forward swing does not begin, however, until the front foot has touched the green. The knees at this point must be bent and relaxed to facilitate the smooth transfer of weight to the front foot. The bowl now comes through, descending under its own weight, with the shoulder, elbow, forearm, wrist and bowl all in perfect alignment with the line of delivery. The bowl is 'grassed' onto the green alongside the front foot and in line with the back foot, with the fingers almost touching the surface at the actual point of grounding. The delivery-hand follows through along the line of the bowl, palm upwards. The head remains still, eyes firmly on the point of aim.

Does orthodoxy matter?

This can be described as a textbook action. In reality, how much should you worry about achieving it? After all, the authors can hardly hold themselves up as models of orthodoxy, although as you will see they do conform to the great absolute – they deliver the bowl time after time in exactly the same manner, which means that they are as much in control of the situation as they can be. They now and again make a hash of a shot, but the fault does not lie with the delivery action.

Having said that, it is surely revealing that neither Allcock nor Bryant recommends his delivery (or that of the other). Their deliveries are far too individualistic to copy successfully, and in the sense

Margaret Johnston of Ireland prepares to bowl from the semi-crouch stance. Hers is a beautifully smooth delivery, like that of so many women bowlers even at club level.

BOWL TO WIN

that you can ever copy anybody, they would point to someone like the New Zealand bowler Peter Belliss, or the highly successful Richard Corsie of Scotland, both of whom possess elegant, flowing deliveries. Even at club level you can hardly fail to notice how beautifully some players, very frequently women, deliver a bowl. It simply comes naturally to them, and while in itself that graceful, almost balletic action does not make them great bowlers, it must count in their favour. In other words, while it is true that natural talent can triumph over eccentric technique, all things being equal, the better the technique the better the bowler.

When it comes to coaching the method of delivery, there are interesting national differences. In the Southern Hemisphere there is a strong belief in uniformity, and if you were to go to clubs the length and breadth of Australia you would see all fit bowlers bowling in much the same manner. In South Africa there is an overwhelming preference for the South African Clinic style. In Britain, however, if you watch 20 players on a green you are likely to see 20 different actions. This does not reflect an anarchistic streak in the British. It is a consequence of the immense diversity of bowling conditions in Britain, and bowlers have quite sensibly taken into account their local conditions in developing their technique. And by and large British coaching methods acknowledge this, placing an emphasis on working with what the player feels most comfortable with rather than trying to impose a uniform, 'correct' style.

There is, at the highest levels of the game, an advantage to the demanding circumstances in which British bowlers must learn their craft. British internationals are more versatile than their opponents, and this shows up in their results. They are successful on all surfaces, anywhere in the world, whereas even the

finest bowlers who have grown up playing on those fast, uniform southern surfaces struggle in the unfamiliar surroundings of an outdoor British green.

THE MECHANICS OF BOWLING

The Australian Ian Taylor (left) mesmerises spectators and fellow bowlers alike with his eccentric delivery – but he does ground the bowl consistently, which is what matters.

This young bowler (below left) displays a highly unorthodox approach to his delivery!

The New Zealander Peter Belliss (right) has long delighted spectators with his classic delivery – a movement that combines grace with effectiveness.

Wrist rotation

If you have watched the authors bowl on television, you may have noticed that while their techniques are in a number of respects radically different, there is one peculiarity they share. Both rotate their bowling arm, first one way during the back swing and then the other way on the forward swing. Why?

Bryant explains: 'In my early years as a bowler, I developed a keen interest in the human anatomy in relation to bowling technique. In particular, I was anxious to discover ways of working within my anatomical limitations to improve the consistency of my delivery. I made the observation that when the arm is swinging freely at the side, the palm invariably faces the leg. In fact, it is only by allowing the arm to pass the leg in this sideways-on position that it is possible for the arm to make the pendulum motion in a straight line, without adjusting the rest of the body

'To see what I mean, stand in the athletic position, feet side by side, and extend both arms behind you, palms facing forwards. Now swing them through past the legs and all the way forward to complete the pendulum swing. Your arms describe an arc, moving noticeably away from the straight by the completion of the swing. To bring your arm through straight when it is locked in this position you must compensate for this anatomical inconvenience by pivoting your hips. Of course if you are using one of the fixed variety of stances your hip pivot is already in place, which means you can bring your arm through straight, but you will bring it through on a different line to the line of the body. In other words, that inescapable hip movement places the arm and the torso out of alignment.

'If you want to avoid this hip movement, in the interests of total body alignment throughout the delivery, you must rotate the wrist so that the arm passes the leg with the palm facing it. I therefore fell naturally into the delivery I use to this day. On the backswing I rotate my wrist so that by the top of the backswing the bowl is facing backwards. Then on the forward swing I rotate my wrist in the opposite direction so that the bowl passes my leg sideways on and, by the point of release, is facing forwards. That way I have managed to keep my entire body in the line of the shot from start to finish.'

Allcock adds: 'I must have picked this up from watching David, although I'm not conscious of having done so. My wrist rotation is less pronounced than his because my backswing is much less full, and I usually only rotate my wrist through 90 degrees, in contrast to the full 180-degree rotation David normally employs. This technique must have come very easily to me or I would never have persisted with it, because however good the theory behind it I am not much influenced by theory. And when you consider that David and I (and to some extent Richard Corsie) are the odd men out among top-class bowlers in bowling this way, you will understand why I still hesitate to recommend it – and certainly don't coach it.'

The wrist rotation employed by both authors is unusual amongst bowlers. It is theoretically sound and feels entirely natural to them, but there is no doubt that it requires perfect timing and is therefore not a technique they recommend.

KEY POINTS
- *Sample a wide variety of bowls before committing yourself.*
- *The biggest bowl you can comfortably handle is probably right*
- *If you have a small hand, consider a heavy weight*
- *Medium bias suits most British conditions*
- *Good shoes are a great investment*
- *There are advantages to both claw and cradle grip, so choose the most comfortable*
- *The grip must be tension free*
- *The athletic stance is the favourite*
- *The feet must point in the line of delivery*
- *A consistent delivery is essential*

THE MECHANICS OF BOWLING

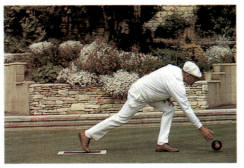

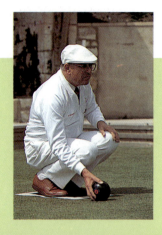

THE BRYANT DELIVERY

I take up my position on the mat sitting on my haunches. In that position my entire body weight is supported by my legs, and I could actually remain in that position for several minutes without experiencing discomfort. In contrast, I find any higher version of the crouch stance puts a strain on the thighs if it is held for any length of time – and I like to take my time. Then, while I weigh the bowl in my hand, holding it in the claw grip, I focus my attention completely on an aiming point along the line I have selected for my shot. I then begin my backswing (with the wrist rotation) as I rise to whatever height experience has taught me is correct for the weight of shot I want to play. So from some version of semi-crouch or athletic stance I bring my arm through, with the reverse wrist rotation, ground the bowl smoothly and follow through with my arm along the line, taking care to keep my head absolutely still right to the end of the follow through. From start to finish my eyes are rivetted on my aiming point.

'This has been my basic delivery for more than 40 years, although recently I have added a slight variation at the beginning. On fast greens I lean forward into what can be described as an extended crouch, and rest the bowl on the green while I am focusing my attention on the point of aim, prior to rising. I find this slightly shortens my backswing, helping me to keep unwanted weight from the shot. At the other end of the scale, when I am in a situation where I want to put maximum controlled power behind a shot, I abandon the crouch altogether, and bowl from an upright stance.

'In addition to the crouch itself and the wrist rotation, there are a few other peculiarities of my delivery. Compared to most, both my backswing and my follow through are somewhat exaggerated, all in aid of that smooth delivery. And the extended follow through often has the effect of taking my back leg well off the mat. While it may sometimes look like I am in danger of losing my balance in this position, I can assure you that it is all under control.

'Viewing my stance and delivery objectively, in the sense of whether it should be used as a model for an aspiring player, it has two big question marks over it. First the crouch. The main reason I adopted it in the first

THE MECHANICS OF BOWLING

place was that I considered – and still consider – that it helps me pick out my line. Line is so important, and my ability to judge it accurately has been so crucial to my success, that I have never felt the need to provide any further justification for the stance. However, bowling that way for such a long time has taken its toll on my knees, and the older I get the more I am reminded of advice I was given at the beginning of my career, when I was told that the crouch was fine for a young man but would become a burden with time. I remain wedded to it – at least for as long as my knees hold out – but the fact that it has gained so few adherents, and that was the case even at the height of my success, speaks volumes.

'Secondly, the wrist rotation. When you watch Tony and me playing together, both employing it, you might gain the impression that it's the most natural thing in the world. It may look that way, but the evidence suggests otherwise. It requires absolutely perfect timing, because the bowl must be perfectly straight in the hand as it is grounded. If you are even fractionally late with it you will over-rotate the wrist and the bowl will come out tilted against the bias, which will ruin the line. Fractionally early and the bowl is tilting inward, with the same result. To get it just right, every time, is essential, and if you cannot do that then the delivery should not be attempted.'

THE ALLCOCK DELIVERY

I have said in print on another occasion that I feel a bit of a fraud discussing my bowling method, on the simple grounds that I don't have one! Worse, I have been embarrassed to find myself describing what I think I do at a particular stage in the delivery only to be contradicted by the evidence on video. This may suggest that I am as confused when I deliver a bowl as I can be when I try to analyse my delivery, but not so. The problem – although it is no problem to me – is that I am a purely instinctive bowler. What talent I have is a natural talent, untutored at any stage, and as far as I am aware uninfluenced by bowling theory.

'When I describe myself as a natural-born bowler I am not straying much from the literal truth. My parents were both county players and my mother represented England. I was, in fact, born between two rounds of a club pairs championship which my mother somehow went on to win! So from my pram I was an observer, apparently a rapt one, of the sport I never remember not loving and wanting to play.

THE MECHANICS OF BOWLING

'As a youngster I inherited an old set of lignum bowls, with which I whiled away happy hours in the back garden – good preparation for the rough, uneven greens I have so frequently encountered during my career! And it was at this time I developed characteristic habits which I persist with to the present day. First, the combination of big lignum bowls and a child's small hands left no option when it came to grip. It had to be the cradle. I still use that most simple of grips on heavy greens or when I want to get real power into the shot, but on quicker greens I make a concession to the need for finer control by moving my thumb up the side of the bowl – the grip we have described as the compromise cradle.

'I naturally began with the athletic stance (no child would do anything else), and that, in its many forms including the semi-crouch, is what I use now, and what I teach to all able-bodied bowlers. So my grip and stance are orthodox, and so is my delivery – up to a point.

'Apart from the wrist rotation, where at least I am in good company in sharing it with David, the aspect of my delivery that has always excited most curiosity is the way I release the bowl and follow through – if you can call it following through. I cannot tell you why I snatch my hand away from the bowl immediately after grounding it, as if I had suddenly put my hand in the fire. I used to argue that I really did have a sort of abbreviated follow through, but the slow-motion camera is obviously not slow enough to pick it up!

'I must have developed this quirk during my backyard bowling days, where I remember being in a tremendous hurry to bowl as many bowls as possible in the available time. Even to this day I don't linger long on the mat. I can defend this wildly unorthodox feature of my delivery only by saying that it has never seemed a problem to me, in the sense that I believe my line is as consistent as anybody else's. If I had ever had any serious problems with line I would have tried to correct my 'fault'. But as the saying goes, 'If it ain't broke, don't fix it!'

'It should hardly need saying that I do not recommend my quick-fire delivery and non-existent follow through to anyone. I coach a completely orthodox delivery, without wrist rotation and complete with follow through. In fact, I try to get my pupils to imagine that there is a steel rod running all the way from the wrist to the shoulder, so keen am I to impress upon them the necessity of bringing the arm absolutely straight through on line. And that, really, is good delivery in a nutshell. If you come through as straight as I do, leg, body and arm all square to the line of shot, that will do nicely.'

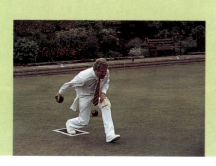 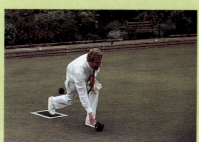 

PLAYING THE SHOTS

2

You do not develop good technique in a vacuum, or in front of a mirror – you do so by bowling, whether on the practice green or under actual match conditions. Fundamental to playing any shot is an adequate command of line and length. Nothing else so rewards accuracy – or punishes inaccuracy. On the basis of good line and length all the shots in the game come within reach.

PLAYING THE SHOTS

FINDING LINE

There is an old saying in bowling circles that the game comes down to the three 'L' words, line, length and luck. There is nothing to be said about the last of these, except to wish you have it, but the other two provide the key to successful bowling. It is no exaggeration to say that any bowler with unvarying mastery of line and length would be unbeatable, and that persistently wayward line and length makes victory impossible. In reality the two are conjoined in a single event, the shot, but it is necessary to view them in isolation for instructional purposes.

The line is the path the bowl takes from the point at which it leaves the hand until it reaches its destination somewhere up the green. The correct line, therefore, is the path the bowl must take to arrive at the destination you have chosen for it. That destination might be another bowl (either your own or your opponent's), a displaced jack or a position on the green selected for tactical considerations, but most of the time it will be the jack in its initial position, centred at a particular length. In discussing the theory of line it is assumed that the last mentioned is the case. The line is the path to the jack.

The bias effect
Clearly the bowl cannot arrive at the jack by correct line alone, but only by the marriage of correct line and correct length. This, however, raises an important point of theory. To get from hand to jack the bowl describes an arc, and that arc is determined by the sideways pull of the bowl (the result of its bias) acting upon its forward momentum. In the early stages of its journey, when the bowl's momentum is at its greatest and the influence of the bias therefore at its

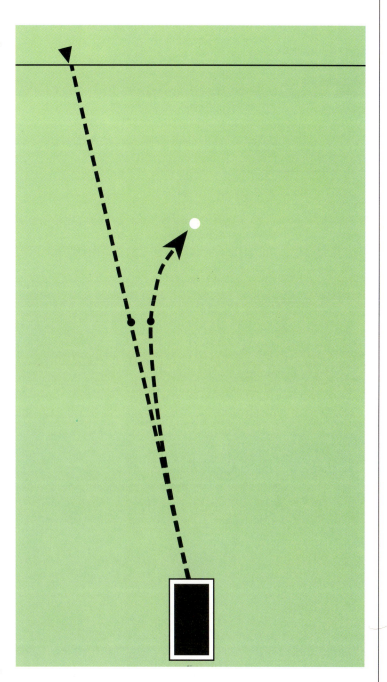

Whether you pick your aiming point on the bank, or bowl to the imaginary shoulder of the arc along the line to such a point, the true shoulder, where the bowl actually turns inward, is necessarily inside the imaginary shoulder.

43

BOWL TO WIN

On a heavy green the arc is relatively narrow and the shoulder relatively close to the mat.

weakest, the arc is comparatively tight. As the bowl runs more slowly in the later stages of its journey so the influence of the bias increases and the arc becomes more noticeable. Hence that peculiar arc – an irregular curve that becomes increasingly pronounced towards the end, as the bowl slows down and homes in (you hope) on its target.

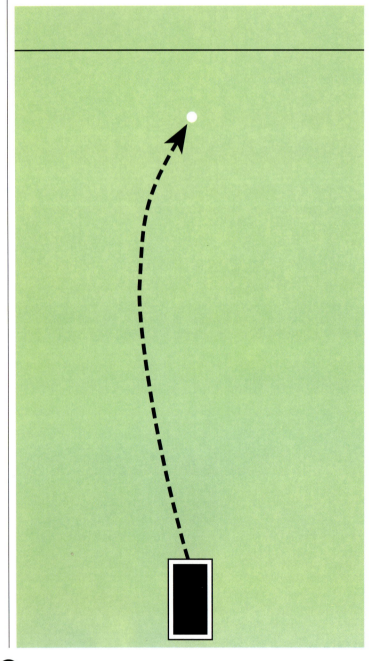

Now imagine three bowls delivered in such a way as to come to rest at different positions along the centreline of the green – say one on the jack, one short and one beyond. In all three cases they got there because the line selected was the line – and the only line – that correctly anticipated the effect of the bias on the running bowl. And because the bias is a constant factor (for that bowl), it follows that the line for each bowl was the same line. It was the weight of shot that took the bowls to different positions along the centreline, but the line did not change. Of course this assumes a green without any vagaries, running perfectly true along its entire surface, and there can never be such a thing. But that does not invalidate this important element of theory. If there were no ditch at the far end, and instead the green stretched on indefinitely, you could in theory bowl at full throttle along the correct line and always come to rest on the centreline. When you realise this you will see that the line to the jack is more accurately described as the line to the centre of the rink, played with jack weight.

The primacy of line

Finding that line, for your bowls, on the rink you are playing, up and down the green, forehand and backhand, must be your number one priority when you first step onto the mat. During the trial ends you will be trying to get a feel for length as well, but if you take a bit of time to find the length it is less serious than being slow to pick out the line. Bowls on line are rarely a complete waste, regardless of length. Good length bowls are pretty well useless if they are seriously off line.

Bowlers vary in their approach to finding line, but in one respect there is unanimity. In order to have a point of aim you have to imagine the bowl's journey, and in particular you have to 'see' it

PLAYING THE SHOTS

begin to curve in towards the jack. The point at which it does this, the widest in the arc the bowl describes, is called the shoulder of the arc. It is generally between two-thirds and three-fifths of the way down the green (in relation to any point on the centreline, remember). If you correctly gauge the shoulder of the arc and get your bowl to it then you are by definition on line.

The most common way of going about this is to extend the imaginary line beyond the shoulder of the arc to a static feature on the bank – a chair perhaps, anything you can see at the end of the imaginary line. That becomes the target to aim at. Alternatively, some players bring the line back to a point on the green nearer the mat, and use that as their aiming point. In theory it makes no difference one way or the other, since the bowl will turn in at the shoulder of the arc regardless. Others prefer to focus their attention on the shoulder of the arc itself, placing something such as an imaginary handkerchief on that spot and bowling over it.

The real shoulder of the arc
However the aiming point is fixed in relation to the shoulder of the arc, you must be aware of the fact that there are in reality two shoulders of the arc – one real, the other imaginary. This may sound a hideous complication, but in practice it is not. The real shoulder of the arc is of course the actual point at which the bowl turns inwards. Now if the bowl travelled in a straight line to that point and then abruptly changed direction you could aim for it. But that is not the case. While you deliver the bowl in a straight line, it starts curving (in response to the bias) from the moment it leaves your hand, so if you were to aim straight for the true shoulder you would inevitably miss it – you would be on a line inside it.

Since you must aim straight at something, what you do is determine the point in a straight line ahead of you that will have the effect of getting the bowl to the true shoulder of the arc. What you are aiming at is the imaginary shoulder of the arc. This imaginary shoulder is always outside the true shoulder, not far outside on a slow green which minimises bias, several feet outside on a fast green which exaggerates it.

On a fast green, the arc is wide, sometimes so wide as to take the bowl into the adjacent rink, and the shoulder is far down the line.

BOWL TO WIN

From his normal crouch David Bryant has a low-level perspective from which to select his line. For drive shots he adopts the athletic stance (for maximum power) and sights the line over the top of the bowl.

THE BRYANT LINE

From the comfort of my normal crouch I have a low-level view of the rink from which to pick out the line that I want. That is the reason for the crouch – I believe it gives me a better perspective for 'seeing' the line. When I am firing from the upright position I hold the bowl out in front of my eyes, as though sighting down a gun barrel. As a rule I like to find my marks on the bank – the white rink boundary markers are a favourite target. Of course it will be pure coincidence if any mark you single out delivers the perfect line, so you must be prepared to make a slight adjustment. The surfaces of outdoor greens provide plenty of visual variety, patches of dry grass or perceptible indentations here and there, and these can make useful marks.

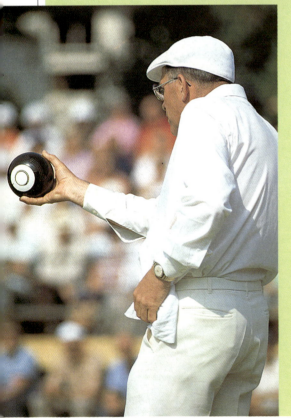

'Players who like to fix on a spot nearer the mat than the shoulder of the arc claim that it allows them to sight the jack while playing the shot. I consider this to be no advantage at all, and personally never look at the jack when bowling. In my opinion, if you look at the jack during the delivery you run the risk of bowling narrow, as a result of an imperceptible shift of line towards the jack. Since the jack has no bearing on the line it is at best an irrelevance, at worst a misleading distraction. The time for looking at the jack is when you are standing on the mat weighing up the shot, weighing the bowl in your hand, determining the strength of delivery required to achieve the desired length. That is when you flick your eyes back and forth between jack and point of aim. Once you come to the point of delivery, however, my advice is to keep your eyes riveted on the aiming point until after the delivery is completed.'

PLAYING THE SHOTS

THE ALLCOCK LINE

'In my youth I used the handkerchief method of locating the shoulder of the arc – literally. I would throw the jack and then place a handkerchief on the spot I reckoned was the shoulder of the arc. Then I would bowl to the handkerchief and note the result. If the handkerchief was correctly placed, the bowl would come to rest on the line of the jack (right on the jack if the weight was right). If not, I would reposition the handkerchief. Once I had it right for that length jack, I would repositon the jack and start again.

'Since in competition you can hardly expect to be allowed to place a handkerchief on the green, I developed my imaginary handkerchief, which I would 'see' quite clearly as I looked down the line. Years on, I seem to have lost the handkerchief, at least as a constant bowling companion. I use it sometimes in the early stages of a game, to get my eye in. Or I may use a mark on the bank. Once I am in the swing of things, though, especially if I am having no difficulty with line, I tend to rely on what I have called my natural orientation. By that I mean that I trust my instinctive feel for where everything on the rink (including me) is in relation to everything else, and I 'see' the line without reference to marks real or imaginary. This is not typical of successful bowlers, and is therefore not to be recommended. Look for your mark and bowl at it.

'As a footnote, because I am not, as a rule, focusing on a mark, I allow my eyes to flicker back and forth between line and jack. Unlike David I do not have a conscious policy about looking at one or the other during the delivery. I think I probably have the jack in sight when I am on a narrow line, at least in the corner of my eye on a medium line, but out of sight on a wide line when it would be unnatural to be looking across my body. Such a flexible approach would be misguided for anyone bowling at a mark.'

From his typical stance Tony Allcock sometimes bowls to the shoulder of the arc, sometimes to a mark on the bank – but often prefers to let his instinctive 'feel' for the situation dictate his line.

47

BOWLING TO LENGTH

Bowling to a desired length is by general consent the most difficult area of the game. With line, once you have found it, unless you are on a really dreadful rink, it will remain pretty constant throughout the match. There will be occasions when you want to deliver a positional bowl off the centreline, and for those shots you will have to determine a new line, either inside or outside the line to the jack, but the technical demands required to achieve this are nothing like as great as those concerning length. Quite apart from the playing conditions of the green, which obviously determine the weight of shot required to achieve the objective, the length of shot is constantly changing. The length of jack varies from end to end. One shot you want to play right to the jack, the next, perhaps, beyond the jack, the third to come to rest alongside an opposition bowl, the last with controlled weight to rearrange the head in your favour. Each of these shots imposes particular conditions on your basic, grooved delivery.

Length is determined by two factors working in opposition: the propulsion you impart to the bowl when you deliver it and the resistance it encounters from the surface over which it is rolling. Because the resistance varies so widely from surface to surface so too must the propulsion, in order to reach the same length on varied surfaces.

In bowling parlance propulsion is known simply as weight of shot, and the factors you need to understand to control weight of shot come right back to stance and delivery. It was stated earlier that the athletic stance is favoured for its versatility, in particular for the ease with which it facilitates changes in weight. If you stand upright on the mat, with your arm swinging freely by your side, you are

Australian Rob Parrella lowers his back leg to the ground, as a means of reducing the weight of shot. This technique is common in the Southern Hemisphere where the fast greens put a premium on delicate shots.

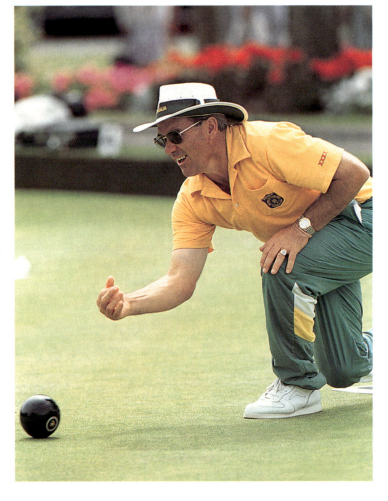

David Bryant demonstrates the long backswing associated with a weighted bowl. The long backswing leads naturally to a long forward step and follow through – the ingredients of weight of shot.

in a position to take a long backswing. A long backswing with its corresponding forward swing gives more unforced weight to a shot than does an equivalent pendulum-like swing starting with a reduced backswing. Moreover, that full backswing leads naturally to a long stride forward during the transference of body weight, and the combined long swing and long step makes for weight of shot. Both those movements create quite naturally another required feature of the heavy shot, which is forward body movement over the bowl, over the front foot as the arm swings through. Finally, this full transference of body weight causes the back foot to lift off the mat, which reinforces the forward momentum.

Easing off on the throttle

Taking that full swing as the starting point, the athletic stance will easily accomodate reduction in weight, by infinitely fine degrees. If you stand a little less erect, leaning forwards slightly or bending the knees, or both, an unforced backswing will be slightly less pronounced, with a knock-on effect right through the delivery, including step, forward body movement and the back leg, which may only rise onto the toes while remaining on the mat. As the athletic stance shades imperceptibly into the semi-crouch so this process continues, with the same natural swing imparting less and less weight to the shot. In effect, it is like the golfer selecting progressively more lofted clubs to achieve shorter distance with the same swing.

For the very gentlest shots, for instance drawing to a short jack on a lightning-quick green, there is a variation to the delivery that is used to great effect in the Southern Hemisphere. As the bowl is delivered off a short backswing the back knee descends to the ground. This drastically curtails the forward body movement and allows for the most delicate control of weight.

Finally, the grip has a role to play in controlling weight. If you use a claw grip you will clasp the bowl firmly as you deliver it with pace. But for 'touch' shots you will ease off on the grip, caressing the bowl as you ground it sweetly. To a lesser extent this is true for the cradle grip as well, although the cradle is a more relaxed method of holding the bowl in the first place.

Regardless of the weight of shot attempted, never curtail the follow through, which is an essential part of even the most delicate of shots. The follow through does not impart weight: it is the final stage in your commitment to following line.

BRYANT ON LENGTH

In discussing any aspect of delivery I always come back to the importance of achieving a smooth, rhythmic action. Too often I have seen players try to control length by concentrating overmuch on one aspect – say the step forward, and that can lead to a jerky delivery. There is a natural relationship between the backswing and the forward step, as there is when you walk, fast or slow. If the height of your stance and the length of your backswing is suited to the pace of the green, the step forward and follow through should come automatically.

'Viewed in terms of length, my own delivery is of the athletic variety, because I rise from the crouch (where I sight line) prior to delivering the bowl. The difference between mine and the conventional delivery from the athletic stance is that I rise into it. The more weight I require, the higher I rise. When I want to drive hard I abandon the crouch altogether.

'Practise that grooved swing until it becomes second nature. Bowling to a fixed jack will hone both line and length. If you can get four bowls close, consistently, then there is nothing wrong with your swing. Move the jack and do it again. String out four jacks along different lengths, from short to full, and deliver a bowl to each. Or bowl to a fixed jack and then take the weight off gradually, shot by shot, yard by yard, always maintaining line. The skills involved here form the basis of your game, and you cannot expend too much effort in trying to master them.'

The extent to which David Bryant rises from his crouch combined with the degree of backswing and corresponding step forward determine weight of shot.

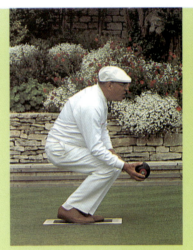

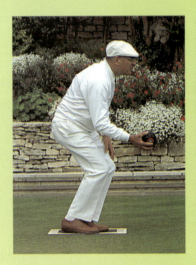

ALLCOCK ON LENGTH

As a youth I practised endlessly to try and perfect both line and length, and in my experience length poses more problems than line. I used to bowl at an imaginary line running horizontally across the green, trying to line the bowls up in a row. Or I would try to string the bowls out in a vertical line, with equal spaces between them. Or, most difficult of all, I would scatter jacks and try to draw a single bowl to each – a searching examination of line and length if ever there was one!

'As for my technique, I'm afraid that once again I rely more on instinct than on theoretical considerations. For example, I must increase my backswing in attempting to put on weight (and videos confirm this), but I'm not conscious of doing so. And my step forward inevitably changes with the backswing. More controversially, I have become aware that I make considerable use of my forearm towards the end of the pendulum swing. I give the bowl a boost at the last moment, the degree of boost governed by my feeling for the length. And I fine-tune that boost with my fingers and wrist, which allows for very subtle gradations of weight. Whether this last second sleight of hand is the cause of my peculiar releasing action or a consequence of it I can't say, but it is unlikely that it will ever find its way into the coaching manual.'

As he does with finding line, Tony Allcock tends to judge length instinctively. This means that backswing and length of step are unconsciously varied in relation to his perception of the shot he has to play. And at the last moment, just as he releases the bowl, he uses his fingers to fine tune the weight of the delivery.

BOWL TO WIN

THE DRAW SHOT

The discussion of bowling on a line and to a length necessarily had a large theoretical component, because insofar as there is a science to bowls it is primarily concerned with how you can maximise your chances of propelling an object accurately from one place to another. And on this there can be endless debate. Where there is no debate, and no necessity for theory, is over the importance of the draw shot. It is by far the most important in the game – justifying its description as the 'bread and butter shot'. If you fail to come to terms with the draw shot you will never be a competent bowler, and it is only by mastering it that you will become a really good one. At the highest levels of the game it is rare for the player who is drawing better than his opponent to lose the match.

Targetting the jack

The reason the draw is so important is, at one level, self-evident. The object of the game is to get your bowl as close to the jack as possible, and for the most part that means drawing to the jack. The draw shot, however, embraces much more than drawing to the jack, even if that is its most common application. Any positional shot is a draw, whether short or long, on the line of the jack or elsewhere on the green, along another line. Then consider all those shots into the head where you are attempting to move an opponent's bowl, promote your own, trail the jack and so on. In each of these cases you take more green, or less, add weight or take it off, and in every case that modification – the more or less – is in relation to the draw. If you cannot bowl to the jack, how can you make the necessary adjustment to bowl just beyond it and a width to the right?

The most elementary of draw shots is the one to an open jack. If you start off playing lead in a team you will have plenty of opportunity to practise it, and there can be no better experience. The first thing a lead has to do is select the

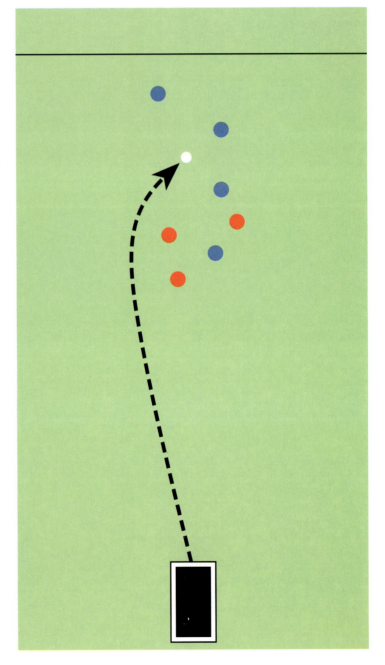

The draw shot to the jack is by far the most important single shot in a bowler's armoury.

52

PLAYING THE SHOTS

truer side of the rink (and one is usually truer than the other, outdoors). Once that choice has been made you should stick to it, bowling forehand one way, backhand the other. Occasionally a rink will be playing truer down one side and up the other, in which case you will want to stick to the appropriate hand, but that is very much the exception to the rule.

This immediately exposes the limitations of relying heavily on one hand or the other. Just as tennis players must be able to cope with playing down either flank, so must bowlers. In reality, while many bowlers display a marked preference for either forehand or backhand, as do tennis players, they have no objejctive reason for doing so. Assuming sound technique, the deliveries are identical, with the leg, body and arm moving directily down the line of delivery. The only obvious difference is between grounding the bowl about a foot outside the mat (forehand) and near the backhand corner of the mat. You should find no greater difficulty in grounding the bowl smoothly on one spot than the other, but if you do initially feel less confident on a particular hand, strive to overcome that feeling. If you allow it to persist it will seriously mar your enjoyment of the game, along with your effectiveness.

Drawing to a displaced jack

While drawing to a fixed jack is the norm during the early stages of an end, as the head builds up the jack is likely to be moved from its spot, often a considerable distance away. Drawing to a displaced jack necessitates an adjustment to line or length, usually both. Assuming you have a good command of both that should not be too difficult, and on an indoor surface (or perfectly uniform outdoor surface, which exists only in the imagination) it is straightforward enough.

However, the realities of outdoor bowling add a slight complication. The grass immediately around the centreline, jack high, is where most of the action takes place, and in the course of the day it gets flattened out both by bowls and feet. If the jack gets moved out into fresh grass the bowl will encounter greater resistance as it gets to it. This means that the line will have to be a little

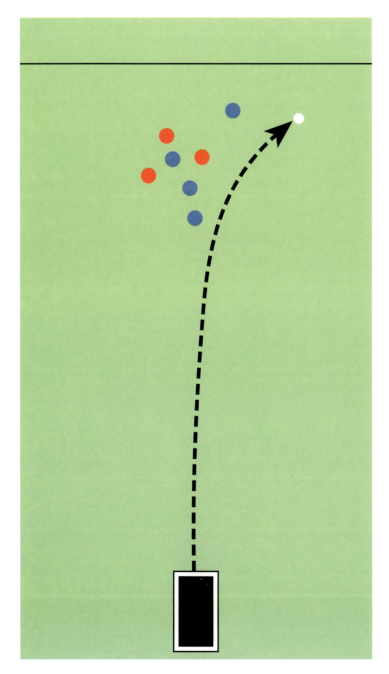

The draw to a displaced jack requires an adjustment either to line or length, and usually both.

BOWL TO WIN

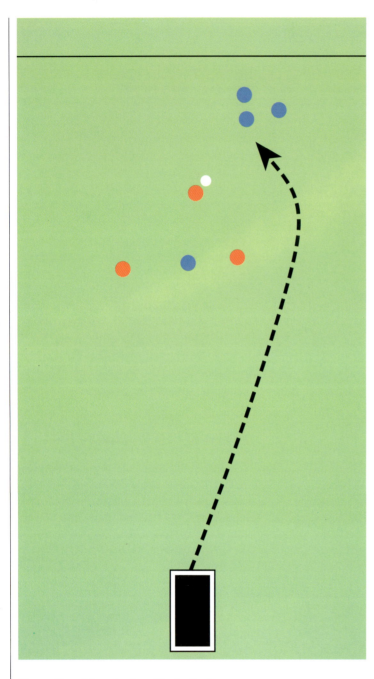

The positional draw is played for tactical purposes (either offensive or defensive). The rest shot (right) has been played to devastating effect, overturning a 3-shot deficit.

tighter than it would otherwise have been (because the bias is less effective on the slower, fresh grass) and the length a little greater (to reach, across the slower grass). On very fast greens this will be a marginal factor, but on a heavy British green this could make a decisive difference to the outcome of the shot.

The positional draw

This term refers to any draw shot that is not directed at the jack – that is, a draw to a particular position on the green, invariably for tactical considerations. There are any number of reasons for playing a positional shot. You may be holding shot and want to cover an opponent's bowl in case the jack is displaced

PLAYING THE SHOTS

in that direction. You may want to protect your own shot bowl by blocking the path to it. Or you may simply want the security of a back bowl in case the jack is driven through the head. Whatever the reason – and scarcely an end goes by without the need for a positional shot – to achieve such a tactical bowl you are again reliant on your drawing ability. From the technical standpoint it is exactly the same as drawing to the jack, with the desired position being substituted for the jack and line and length adjusted accordingly.

Recurring positions

Two positional draws are so common a feature of the game that they merit a name: the rest shot and the blocker.

The rest shot is a delicate variation of the draw employed when the jack is less accessible than the opponent's shot bowl. The shot bowl becomes the substitute jack, the aim being to come right up and 'rest' against it on the inside (nearer the jack). A noteworthy attraction of the rest shot is that a bowl presents a far larger target for the draw than a jack does.

The blocker can be an invaluable weapon, and will often transform an end. It is a short bowl intended to impede the opponent's approach into the head, and is commonly used when the head is in your favour but is vulnerable to counter-attack. The blocker can be positioned just short of the head, where it is most effective against the draw, or well short of the head, to counter the threat of a drive. Wherever it is played, accurate line is essential, and a poorly-executed blocker is a wasted bowl.

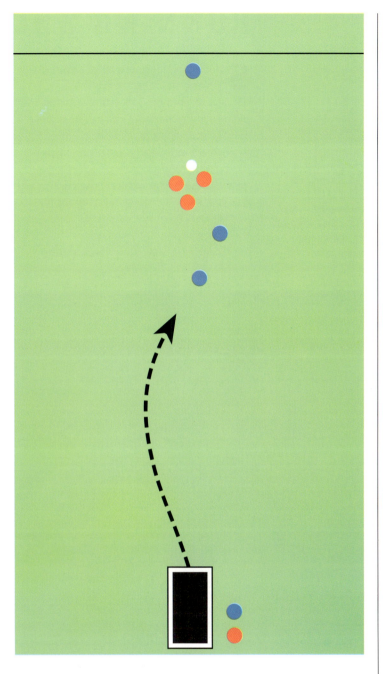

The blocker or block shot is a defensive positional draw, the purpose being to obstruct an opposition bowl from entering the head. The well-placed blocker can provide very effective protection against a drive.

BOWL TO WIN

RUNNING SHOTS

A running shot is any bowl played with significantly more than draw weight – from the delicate yard-on type shots to the fiercest drives.

Strictly speaking, any shot played with greater than draw weight is a running shot, although at the gentler end of the spectrum the running shots have almost everything in common with the draw itself and little in common with the full-blooded drive or firing shot. As you would expect, the shots in the middle of the spectrum combine features of both. For clarity's sake it is desirable to group the various running shots under three headings, although it will be apparent that at the margins separating them the distinction between the types of shot is merely one of nomenclature. The three types of running shot are:

1 The yard-on shot and all its close relations that require just a little added weight.
2 Firm woods, which require stepping up a gear.
3 Driving shots, which may vary in weight but are unmistakably aggressive in intent.

PLAYING THE SHOTS

The yard-on shot

This can be a confusing term because of its implied precision – a shot played with a yard more than draw weight. In fact a good case could be made for striking the term from the bowling vocabulary for precisely this reason. It is common to see a skip indicate an opposition bowl which he wants removed and request a yard-on shot, when in reality to achieve the result the shot must be played with, say, two yards of extra weight. The skip may know this, and presumably he hopes his team-mate knows it too, and will interpet the instruction accordingly. In other words, he says 'yard-on' but really means 'sufficient weight to shift the offending bowl out of the way'. That is a very imprecise way of giving an instruction.

The rescue shot

The yard-on is usually deployed as a rescue shot, when the head is against you but still salvageable. It may be the preferred option even where there is a clear draw to the jack, if, for example, you hold second wood (or more), and need only remove the shot bowl and stay near to make a substantial count. In that instance the rescue act, if achieved, turns out to be a positive blow as well.

To execute any running shot you must allow for the fact that an increase in pace cuts down on the effect of bias, so they are always straighter than the draw, more or less. For the yard-on it is only a little straighter, on heavy greens. On very fast greens, even a yard of extra weight requires a significant adjustment to line, and these delicate running shots become fiendishly difficult to control accurately. Consequently, while they are very much the common currency of British bowls, they figure little in the Southern Hemisphere, where the draw and the drive predominate.

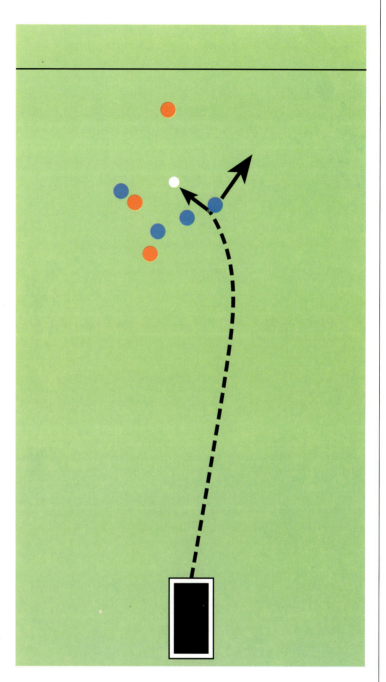

As the name implies, the yard-on shot is played with a yard more than draw weight. The term is often used imprecisely, to indicate 'a little running', but the good skip will refrain from such a lazy instruction.

BOWL TO WIN

Tap and lie

If we accept the convention of the yard-on as a weighted bowl with anything between a yard and two yards running (with the proviso that the skip should take the trouble to spell out the distance accurately), the tap and lie is a light yard-on, with about two feet of running. The aim of this shot is to 'tap' the object bowl out of the way delicately enough to 'lie' in the position vacated. Its alternative name is the wrest shot, because the object is to 'wrest' possession of the object bowl's position. The object is usually an opposition bowl holding shot, but not necessarily. It may be your own shot bowl, and the tap and lie your means of building a count. That gifted, and much loved, Scottish bowler, the late Willie McQueen, was a master of it. He was known by his opponents as 'the machine', for the way he would just tap and and lie, tap and lie, either replacing the opponent's bowl or clustering his own around the jack for a big tally.

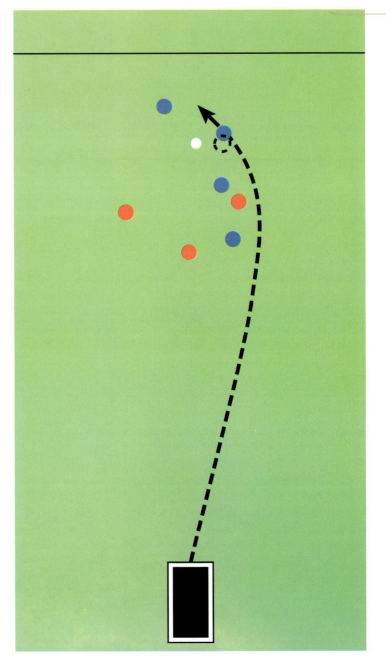

The tap and lie shot is played with slightly less than a yard of running, the aim being to replace the object bowl with the bowl delivered. Here, the shot bowl and jack present an inviting target for such a shot.

PLAYING THE SHOTS

It is no surprise that a Scot should be a great exponent of this shot, for it favours heavy greens – and they do not come any heavier than in Scotland. There is more margin for error on a slow green, and the tap and lie takes advantage of this. As long as it stays the course (and it should, with a couple of feet of running), it will, if it is on line, at least reach its target, if only as a rest shot. It tends not to matter much if it barely dislodges the object bowl or sends it a bit further through. If your line lets you down and you miss, assuming you have reasonable weight you should be left with a useful bowl in the head. As a head progresses, the tap and lie often supplants the draw, which requires greater accuracy.

The tap and lie comes into its own in the later stages of an end, when the head becomes cluttered.

Trailing the jack

This involves bowling to the jack with enough added weight to pick the jack up and 'trail' it to some other location, either further back in the head or all the way to the ditch (when it becomes a firm wood or a driving shot). The trail is generally reckoned the most difficult shot in the game, because the jack is such a tiny target in comparison to a bowl. Not only is such pinpoint accuracy extremely difficult, even for the most accomplished bowlers, but a near miss can be infinitely worse than the proverbial miss by a mile. If instead of picking up the jack cleanly you deal it a glancing blow, you may slice it straight towards a waiting opposition bowl: the very last result that you want.

This shot must therefore be approached with considerable circumspection – it may often be an option, but it is not often the best option. The trail is usually reserved for the later stages of the end (in particular as a last shot), when your opponent is holding shot but you have bowls clustered behind the jack. A draw on your final bowl would save the end, but a successful trail would give you a count. An alternative scenario might be where the head has built in such a way that you have a strong position on one side, while your your opponent is strong on the other side. Whether or not you are holding shot, it might possibly be advisable to trail the jack

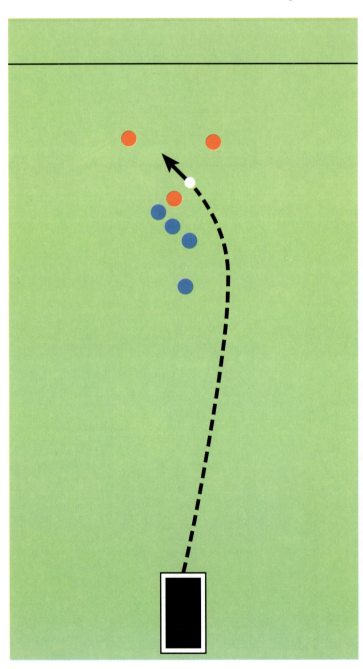

PLAYING THE SHOTS

towards your strength, rather than wait for your opponent to attempt the same thing. Or your shot bowl might be right alongside the jack and jack high – one of the worst of all positions in bowls since it presents such an inviting target to your opponent, who only has to draw with a little added weight. However, if you can trail the jack around the corner ('tucking the jack'), you should hold a much better shot, with the bowl that was shot now affording you some protection, and giving you more hope.

Picking the spot
With all slightly-weighted shots it is possible to envisage them as positional draws, with the position being the spot the bowl would arrive at if its journey were unimpeded. Pick that spot, find the shoulder that provides a line to it, judge the weight and draw. In theory any shot, even the most weighted, can be imagined this way, since they all must run out of steam eventually, but it is hardly practicable to draw to an imaginary point far beyond the ditch! With the delicate shots it is feasible, however, and it is the right way to play the trail because a jack struck flush will travel about as far as the bowl would have travelled as a pure draw. So if you decide where you want the jack to come to rest and bowl to that position on a line running through the jack, you will make the shot. In practice that means tightening your line slightly and putting a yard or so of weight on to your bowl.

The purpose of the trail (below, far left) is to remove the jack to a more advantageous position. That may be a few feet behind – or all the way to the ditch.

Welsh International Brian Kingdon leaves skip, Spencer Wilshire, in no doubt about what a super trail shot he has pulled off. The trail is considered so difficult because the jack presents such a small target, but when it succeeds it can utterly transform an end.

BOWL TO WIN

The wick and plant

The wick is a ricochet shot, where the bowl comes into the head, caroms off another bowl and (maybe) approaches the jack by this circuitous route. It is exactly the same as a cannon in snooker parlance, and like the cannon it is apt to raise eyebrows if it produces a favourable result. A lot of wick shots are flukes, and even when they are not, spectators – and your opponent – will probably view them as such. No matter. If the jack cannot be approached directly, and if there is a realistic chance of wicking onto it, then you should certainly consider this option. The most favourable circumstance is where two or more bowls are tight together in the head, sitting in such a way that a ricochet in the right direction is the likely outcome of getting in amongst them. The wick is best suited to a medium-pace green. On a very heavy green you may get insufficient rebound, whereas on a fast green the wick suffers from the usual yard-on liabilities. Finally, it is useful to note that the wick will have the effect of increasing or decreasing your bowl's arc, depending upon whether it strikes the target bowl on its own bias side or non-bias side.

Assessing the downside
Before attempting a wick, weigh the odds. It is unlikely that you would be tempted by it if the head were in your favour. However, even if the head is against you, what you must consider with such a chancy shot is the likely consequence of failure. If you see a distinct possibility that a botched attempt would disturb the head in such a way as to worsen your plight (by driving the target bowl towards the jack, for instance), then look for a less risky way of extricating yourself. Remember the old snooker proverb: 'It's not what you make; it's what you leave!'

The snooker analogy continues with the plant, where the two games share the term. If two bowls are actually touch-

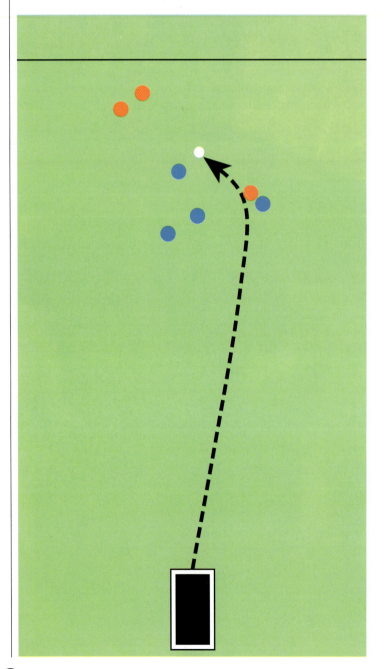

The wick can be a spectacular shot (whether played deliberately or a fluke result). When the route to the head is blocked, it is worth checking to see if two or more bowls are clustered in such a way as to make a wick feasible.

PLAYING THE SHOTS

ing, striking one will propel the other in a predictable direction. Wherever you make contact with the first bowl, the second will take off straight along the line in which it was placed in relation to the first. You see snooker players looking for plants all the time, and as a bowler you should do so too. Admittedly it is much easier to play a plant in snooker, since there is no difficulty in getting the cue ball to strike the touching pair, but if a plant is 'on' in bowls consider it carefully. It can be ideal either for promoting your own bowl or for getting rid of an opponent's. Remember that if the two bowls are not actually touching the plant loses its predictability, which is its great attraction, and as they become further apart the chances of driving one onto the other at the correct angle become slim. Mutterings about a flukey result are perhaps not unwarranted when the plant at a distance materialises.

The shot within a shot

The thing to remember with these and other shots into a mature head is that they can be viewed as second choices. They are basically yard-on shots, and when you look at the head and work out what to play, consider the consequences of a near miss. If you have two alternatives of roughly equal difficulty, say one on either hand, which shot is likely to turn out to be useful in some other way if it fails in its immediate purpose? Which yard-on, missing by a width, could convert into a useful wick? If you take that into account when selecting your shot, is the resulting wick really a fluke?

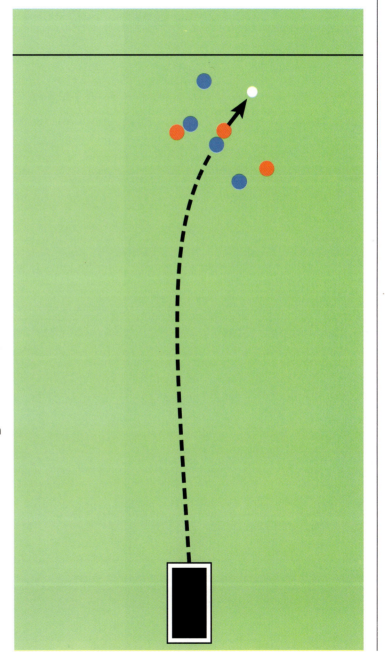

Even more than the wick, the successful plant requires a specific arrangement of bowls in the head. But touching bowls in the correct alignment make the plant very much 'on'.

FIRM WOODS

Between those delicate, or comparatively delicate, running shots and the drive there lies a huge range of possible weights. The firm woods, sometimes called timing shots, are all those shots played with substantial but controlled weight. The aim can be to take out an opponent's bowl, promote your own or to shake up a head that is unfavourable. Whether it is a shot with several yards of weight or a semi-drive, for example trailing the jack to the ditch, the principle of delivery is the same. The key point is that the weight is controlled, and there is some allowance for bias.

One of the most effective firm woods is the run-through, where the head is closed, with short bowls barring your way through to the jack. If you can come into those short bowls with several yards of running you should scatter them, and find your own bowl running through for a yard or so, which can transform the head in your favour. This can be spectacularly effective where there are two blocking bowls side by side, not touching but without sufficient space to get between them. If you can hit the gap or the inside of either bowl (a big target) you will split

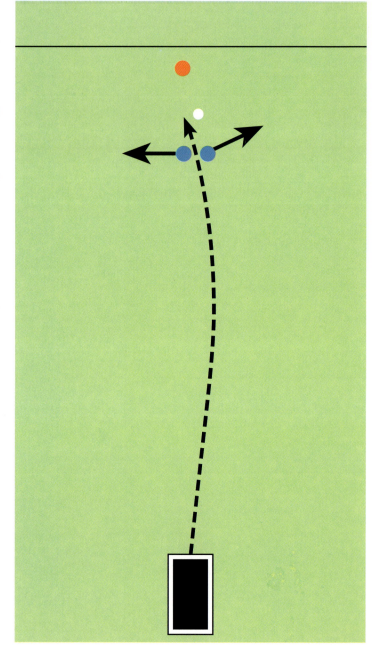

them and run sweetly through in a straight line. You must, of course, be able to prejudge the amount of running required to achieve the desired run-through, and narrow your grass accordingly to get the right line.

Firm woods are much favoured in Britain because the line is tighter and the weight more easily gauged on a heavy green. And when you might prefer a drive but have no direct path to your target, the firm wood may take just enough green to allow you to swing round the obstacle. Like the yard on, the firm wood does not feature largely in the Southern Hemisphere.

One final consideration: wherever possible, when you are trying to take a bowl out of the head, attack it from the hand that swings away from the head rather than towards the head. If you are swinging across the head and out, even imperfect contact will propel the target bowl away from the head. If the same thing happens when you are swinging across but in, you could regret it.

Tony Allcock moves sharpish to get out of the way of a firmly-weighted bowl. The significant difference between the firm wood and the firing shot is that the firm wood is not played with sufficient weight to negate bias completely (or nearly completely, as the drive does). It can therefore bend round an obstructing bowl (to an extent, depending on the degree of obstruction and the pace at which the shot is played).

BOWL TO WIN

THE DRIVE

The most spectacular shot in the bowler's armoury is also the most controversial. As little as a generation ago the drive was rather frowned upon in Britain – a vulgar display of raw power, even unsporting. In clubs today you can still encounter similar distaste for the drive, certainly if it is employed routinely rather than in exceptional circumstances.

It must be admitted that an over-reliance on the drive does not make for attractive bowls, but it is perhaps more relevant to point out that it does not make for successful bowls either. It is difficult to drive accurately, and unless you can you will lose far more matches by driving badly than you will ever win by driving well. Even the best exponents of the drive will admit that they win more by drawing than driving. And, while it is a counsel of perfection, if you play all the touch shots well enough you should not have to fall back on the drive very often. Nevertheless, there are situations where the drive is the best available option, and if you become proficient at it you will have a valuable weapon to hand.

A last resort
The drive is essentially a rescue shot, often your last line of defence when the head is set against you and there is nothing useful you can realistically hope to achieve by playing any other shot. Say you are several shots down and there is no way that a draw can significantly lower that count against you. There are several favourable outcomes that could result from a drive. Best of all, you might be able to displace your opponent's counters and spring the jack for a trail, taking shot or even, if the gods are really smiling, ending up with a count yourself. More realistically, you might ditch the jack and follow it in, or take the jack out of the confines of the rink and kill the end – an excellent result when you are facing a count. Even if that lies beyond the scope of your drive, you may get rid of some of the shots ranged against you, reducing the deficit.

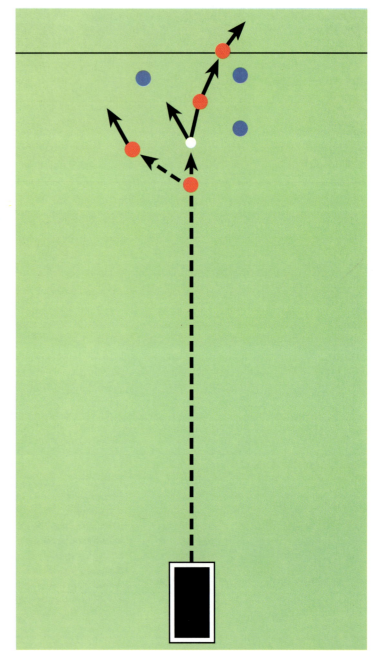

Rob Parrella (right) prepares to drive – and he is one of the fiercest exponents of the shot.

PLAYING THE SHOTS

KEY POINTS
- **To establish and keep to line you need a point of aim**
- **The imaginary shoulder of the arc always lies outside the real shoulder**
- **Length is more difficult than line because it is more varied**
- **Length of backswing controls length of shot**
- **The faster the green, the more difficult length becomes**
- **The draw is the most important single shot – by far**
- **An inaccurate blocker is a wasted bowl**
- **Yard-on type shots are extremely difficult to play on fast greens**
- **Firm shots are more suited to heavy greens**
- **The drive should generally be viewed as a last resort**

Because of the unpredictability of the outcome, it is important not to rush into the drive without weighing all alternatives. For example, it is generally not a good idea to drive if you are only a single shot down. Even if you have a couple of second woods, you might hit them instead and go down by a handful. Again, if you can draw a saving shot (even if it does not give you shot itself), that is the more prudent course of action. A conservative draw will not leave you worse off. A flamboyant drive may very well do so.

Having emphasised the 'last resort' element in the decision to drive, it should be said that there are occasions when a drive is used constructively. If an opposition bowl is isolated from the head but still a menace (second wood, say), it might be safer to drive it out rather than go for a firm wood, to avoid the risk of a mishit inadvertently sending the target bowl towards the head. Here the analogy is with cricket, where the saying goes, 'if you are going to flash, flash hard', so that if you get an edge it will clear the slips.

Another example is where your opponent may have shots around the jack but nothing in front, in which case if you attempt to drive the jack to the ditch and miss, you should clear out one or more of his bowls.

The drive is aimed straight at the target, and so must be delivered with sufficient pace to nullify the effect of bias. That is the theory. In practice, on a heavy green with a full-length jack it may be impossible to generate enough pace to kill the bias entirely, so you will have to take a slight amount of green. The more green you have to take, the less the shot is a true drive and shades toward the firm wood. Here, for once, the fast green favours the shot, because the bowl maintains its speed longer and that speed counteracts bias. Not surprisingly, along with the draw, the drive is the favourite shot amongst bowlers from the Southern Hemisphere. The Australian Rob Parrella can send the jack flying into the crowd, and has been known to shatter an opponent's bowl.

THE TACTICAL GAME 3

There have been many references in preceding pages to tactics, in the context of the types of shot and the situations to which they are appropriate. The subject of bowls tactics generally is a wide one, because it covers every decision you make in the course of a match. In broad terms, the tactics of any game of skill are easy to comprehend. In the case of bowls, it is a matter of building the head, in every end, in such a way as to minimise the chances of your opponent achieving final advantage, and maximise your chances of doing the same. As the match proceeds other factors will come into play, such as who is winning, at what stage, and by what margin, but that does not alter the fact that as you begin each end you are setting out to outbowl your opponent. To do that, you must apply your bowling skills within the ever-changing dynamics of the match. Tactics can be viewed, in this light, as the application of skills to the realities of the moment. In practice this means shot selection, for it is the only area of the game completely under your control. And astute shot selection can only be based on an accurate appraisal of all the relevant factors that are not within your control.

THE TACTICAL GAME

The authors deep in thought, oblivious to the looming television camera – or anything else. They are pondering the choice of shot, the essence of tactical play.

GREENSPEED

There have been earlier mentions of the speed at which various greens play, usually by way of contrasting conditions in Britain with those in the Southern Hemisphere. Although greenkeeping plays a part, this is mainly a matter of climate, with the speed of British greens reflecting the higher rainfall and and lower sunshine levels which are their lot. However, while it is perfectly sensible to describe this green as slow, and that one as quick, these are comparative terms. A very quick green in Britain would be as slow as a New Zealander would be likely to encounter at home, and vice versa. It is useful to have an objective way of describing the slowness or quickness.

The convention is to describe the greenspeed in seconds – the number of seconds it takes a bowl to draw from mat to jack (taken for the purposes of this calculation as a standard 30 yards). So it is that you have a 9-second green (dead slow) and a 27-second green (very fast indeed). It may seem paradoxical that on the fast green the journey time is treble what it is on the slow green, but it is not. That journey time is the time it takes to draw to the jack, not drive it. On the slow green the resistance the bowl encounters is comparatively high, so it must be delivered with considerable force if it is to last the distance. It sets off at speed, therefore covering most of its journey quite quickly, then slows dramatically towards the end. On the fast green the bowl meets much less resistance, so it must be delivered with less force. It sets off comparatively slowly and almost dawdles along, gradually losing speed until it crawls up to the jack. Even a tiny excess of weight will cause the bowl to finish distressingly long. So it is that short journey-time equates with slow green, long journey-time with quick green.

The examples quoted (9 and 27 seconds) are pretty near the extremes encountered. Even the most ill-prepared British green at the beginning of the

The quicker the green, the slower the journey and the wider the arc.

17 seconds

9 seconds

THE TACTICAL GAME

season, after a wet winter, is unlikely to play slower than 7 or 8 seconds. If they did you would be hard-pressed to drive the ditch! And at the height of the New Zealand summer, when the fastest greens in the world play like polished glass, claimed greenspeeds of 30 seconds and more have a mythical ring. Even in the high 20s you find you have to bowl well into the adjacent rink to draw the jack! Commonly, British greenspeeds are just into double figures, although during a very hot summer they can reach the high teens, while in the Southern Hemisphere around 18-22 seconds is typical. Indoor rinks naturally fluctuate within a much narrower band, usually around the 15-second mark.

A daily reading
Australian greenkeepers try to take the guesswork out of reading the speed by measuring the speed each morning and posting the result. It may be helpful to be told that yesterday's 16-second green is today's 18-second, but the fact remains that the greenspeed is what it is, and the trial ends are there for you to adjust yourself to it. In Britain, any such well-intended help would be downright confusing, because of the vagaries of a normal day's weather. On a sunny day the greenspeed picks up as the morning dew dries, reaching its maximum during the heat of the afternoon, and then slows down again as evening approaches. A sudden shower will have a dramatic effect. Even a spell of cloud cover will make a noticeable difference. There is no external agency that could possibly help you under such circumstances. You must observe the changing realities of the moment with hawk-like keenness, and adjust your bowling to them. If you are only fractionally quicker off the mark than your opponent in this respect you will have gained an advantage.

Finally, you must be careful not to fall into the trap of anticipating the probable result of a change in conditions. For example, after heavy rain a green may start off in the morning so wet that the bowls fairly skim along on a film of water. Then as the sun goes to work, drying up that surface film but drawing the underlying dampness to the surface, the slick, quick surface may become sodden and slow.

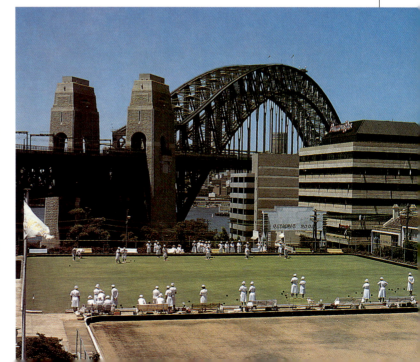

The sight of water indicates a heavy green – whereas the sight of Sydney Harbour Bridge indicates a quick one!

THE WIND FACTOR

A bowl is sufficiently heavy to be unaffected by light breezes, but strong winds are a bowler's nightmare. Worst are those squally conditions where it is dead calm one moment, whipping up a gale the next. Of course you will try to make your deliveries during a lull, but that is not always possible. Strong headwinds or tailwinds completely invalidate greenspeed calculations and necessitate instant adjustments to length. Sidewinds play havoc with line, either accentuating or countering the bias. As a general policy it is advisable to stick to the widened hand (tacking into the wind, as it were), because the wind will then be assisting your bowl during the final stages of its journey. There can be exceptions to this, if, for example, one side of the green is showing more consistency than the other. And consistency is what you must strive for under these trying circumstances. Bowl the hand that yields the most consistent results.

Fluttering flags provide the evidence for wind here – and so too will the behaviour of the bowls in anything much above light breezes. Strong head- or tailwinds radically affect greenspeed (and therefore length), while sidewinds affect the bias (and therefore line).

THE TACTICAL GAME

THE HUMAN FACTOR

A bowling green requires considerable care and attention to keep it in prime condition. The high costs of greenkeeping have resulted in a general deterioration in green standards during the modern era.

While the elements will always have a huge influence on day-to-day bowling conditions, they do not bear that burden alone. As with any sport played out of doors on a prepared surface, the maintenance of that surface is a serious matter. An instructional manual is no place for a prolonged discussion of the state of contemporary greenkeeping, but the authors feel strongly that the bowling community should at least be aware of the simple realities. In the course of their long careers they have witnessed a steady decline in the overall standards of greenkeeping in the British Isles. This is not nostalgia, not a backwards look through rose-tinted spectacles, but a matter of unarguable fact.

A generation or two ago any bowling club that considered itself worthy of the name enjoyed the services of a full-time greenkeeper. Labour was comparatively cheap then, so it was possible to combine top-class maintenance with modest club fees. That is no longer the case, and when faced with the choice between high standards (at a price) and the inexpensive enjoyment of their sport,

THE TACTICAL GAME

bowlers have, pretty decisively, opted for the latter. An understandable choice, perhaps, but there is no getting away from the fact that it results in mediocre standards of greenkeeping that frequently deteriorate to the deplorable. And as the requirement for professional greenkeeping declines, so too does the wealth of specialist skills that made up the greenkeeper's art. The time may come (has come?) when the beautifully-presented British green in high summer retreats into the mists of memory.

At the very end of the season, a conscientious greenkeeper extracts cores from the green and fills them in with top dressing and/or sand. This practice, called hollow tining, aids aeration of the soil, improves drainage and stimulates growth.

Apart from the maintenance, or lack of maintenance, of the green, there are many human factors that impinge on bowling conditions. Where greens are artificially watered, one part may get more of a drenching than its neighbour, and if they lie within the same rink that will make a difference. If on a given day one side of a rink is heavily favoured by bowlers it will become worn and therefore faster. Longer-term wear and tear is another consideration. As the strings are moved in an attempt to ensure uniformity of usage over time, you are always likely to find one part of the rink more worn than another. Heavy wear is especially noticeable around the sides of the green, with ditch rinks having been so well-trodden before the switch in rink direction brought them into play.

Depending upon how well the green has been tended, a degree of tracking will become noticeable in the course of a day's play. Tracking occurs along the principal lines of play where the weight of continuous traffic flattens the grass. It is more of a problem on heavy greens, particularly if they have not been closely cut, and can result in the creation of a perceptible groove (or grooves). Because tracking is inevitable you must be alert to it, and make suitable use of mat and jack positioning so as to turn the developing situation to your advantage.

USE OF MAT AND JACK

In a sense the mat and jack are neutral participants in the game, being common to both sides. However, the laws of bowls have been designed to create an important tactical role for these neutrals, and a match may easily turn on exploiting the opportunities provided. The rules are quite cunning. At the beginning of a game the mat must be centred on the rink, with its leading edge six feet (1.83m) from the the ditch. Thereafter, the player bowling first (the winner of the last scoring end) may move the mat along the centreline anywhere up the rink to a point not less than 76 feet (23.16m) from the front ditch. The mat, once placed, remains in that position for the end.

The jack is cast by the player bowling first, and is delivered from the mat just like a bowl. It must come to rest within the confines of the rink no less than 70 feet (21.33m) from the front of the mat. It is then centred at that length, unless it is less than six feet from the front ditch, in which case it is deemed a full-length jack and is centred on that six-foot mark. The significant implication of these stipulations is that when the mat is fully forward only a full-length jack will do. Anything less will not be 70 feet from the front of the mat, and the jack is then handed to an opponent.

It will be apparent that these laws place a premium on being able to deliver the jack with finely-controlled length. Line should not pose a problem because the jack is unbiased and runs straight – it takes an embarrassingly poor delivery to send the jack scuttling across into an adjoining rink! But length is critical if you want to take full advantage of the potential for mat movement. If you cannot be confident of delivering a full-length jack, you are inhibited from taking the mat right up the green – a significant limitation. And from any mat position, you must be confident that the shortest jack you cast will travel the stipulated 70 feet.

Delivering the jack is straightforward. Stand on the mat with your feet facing

The mat has a fixed position for the opening end. Thereafter, it becomes a tactical weapon.

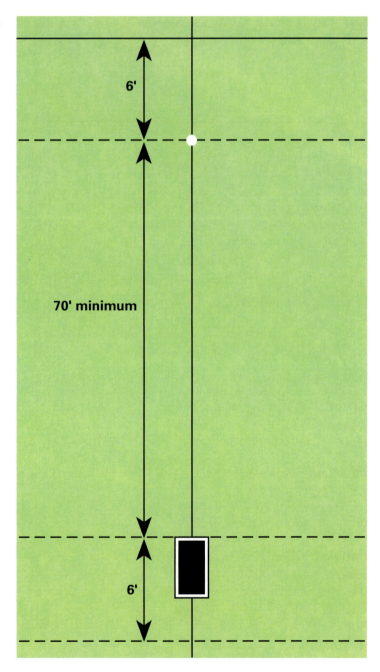

THE TACTICAL GAME

the line (in this case right down the centreline) and bowl as you would for a draw shot. Some players prefer to hold a bowl in the other hand while they cast the jack, the idea being that they retain a feeling for length when they then simply have to transfer the first bowl from hand to hand, rather than interrupt themselves by stooping down to pick up a bowl. There is nothing to be said against this, but neither Allcock nor Bryant does it.

To bowl first – or last?

The first tactical decision taken in any game is whether or not to take the jack if you win the toss. There are advantages and disadvantages to doing so, and the bowler is not conditioned to take first jack automatically, as the tennis player routinely accepts the opportunity to serve first. For if you bowl first, your opponent bowls last. You must therefore weigh the advantage of setting the length against the advantage of holding last bowl.

In a team game, there is a good case for relinquishing the jack in favour of the final bowl. In the trial ends the leads will have had only four bowls apiece, and are unlikely to have got sufficient feel of the green to have developed a significant preference for a particular length. On the whole the real advantage of the skip's being able to convert the head with a final bowl outweighs the theoretical advantage of setting the length.

In singles play, there is on balance a better case for taking the jack. You will have had the opportunity to play eight shots during the trial ends and may well have noticed something about the green or about your opponent's reaction to it. In that case there is much to be said for setting the length and getting your bowl close, because if you do that you are likely to be in the driving seat for that end and be first off the mark.

There are other considerations which can outweigh those general preferences.

Maybe your team has a real flair for long jacks, in which case why not seize the chance to start on a full length? If you win that first end you can repeat the exercise in the second, and thereafter as long as you do not drop an end. Or you might be aware of an opposing team's fondness for long jacks, in which case might it not be a good idea to unsettle them right at the outset by forcing them to play to less than a full length? In singles play, perhaps you come away from the trial ends with less of a feel for the green than you would like, or maybe just feeling 'cold'. Why not let your opponent get on with it, and hope that you will have got into the rhythm of things by the time you come to play that last bowl, which can always transform the outcome?

The jack is delivered exactly like a bowl, from either the claw or cradle grip as the bowler prefers – although the claw is much more widely favoured.

BOWL TO WIN

To deliver the jack, take up your position on the mat exactly as you would to deliver a bowl. Then go through the complete bowling action, including the smooth follow through. What you are aiming to do is place the jack to a predetermined length, not just lob it vaguely up the rink.

Finally, there is the case of the extra end, and whether to accept the jack. This can be an even trickier call to make. By now everyone is familiar with the green, and familiar too with the opposition. You know that your team has been playing well to this length and their's to that, that your lead is drawing more consistently than theirs, or the reverse, that you as skip have been really telling with your final bowls, or not. There are endlessly conflicting factors at play here, and it is impossible in the abstract to come down in favour of the jack or the last bowl.

Turning from the consideration of first jack to the tactical positioning of the jack at other times during the game, there are one or two general observations that do not involve the related use of the mat. If your opposition is inexperienced, or an unknown quantity, it is a good idea to test them with full-length jacks. Inexperienced bowlers tend to be wary of the ditch, and therefore are likely to come up short. Until you have evidence to the contrary, have the confidence in your game to assume that you will gain more than you lose by setting up heads near the ditch. And if you or your team really are superior, you will on the whole maximise your advantage by playing to a full length, because that encourages the skilful touch shots that demand finely-judged weight. If, on the other hand, you find yourself up against superior forces, you will want to do everything you can to position the jack so as to neutralise the opposition's advantage.

It is when the jack is viewed in conjunction with the mat that the full tactical implications unfold. There are two reasons for moving the mat. You do so either to position it where it suits you or where it does not suit the opposition. While these twin objectives may be achieved simultaneously, that can only be by happy coincidence, so the two tactics should be examined individually.

When you move the mat, you alter the playing surface, to a greater or lesser extent. For the sake of your own bowls

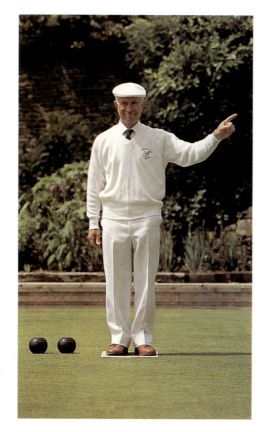

The bowler indicates to the marker the direction to move the jack in order to centre it. The upraised arm indicates that it is dead centre.

you may want to do this because you are having difficulty with length, or some tracking is interfering with your line. There may be surface imperfections that you would like to avoid. Or you may simply feel very comfortable, say, bowling short to a full-length jack (a testing combination). Whatever, a particular stretch of the rink may be your favourite for the game, and all things being equal you would naturally prefer to play it whenever you have the opportunity to do so.

Tony Allcock prepares to deliver the jack, holding a bowl in his left hand. In practice neither Allcock nor Bryant does this, but some bowlers claim that it helps not to have to pick up a bowl after delivering the jack.

Moving the mat down the rink is a tactical ploy.

Making it easy on yourself is not, however, the only consideration, maybe not even the most important one. Your aim is to make things as uncomfortable as possible for the opposition. You may have noticed that they have a decided preference for one position and length or a dread of another, and you will want to exploit this, even if it puts a strain on your own bowling. For example, if you are playing well from a particular mat position only to discover that the opposition likes it even better (as witness the scorecard), there is little point in persisting with it. Conversely, a mat position that is merely difficult for you may be quite hopeless for them, in which case you should grit your teeth and stick to it. Or it may be that frequent changes of mat upset your line and length less than they do the opposition's, in which case you have something to gain by mixing it up as much as possible. And so on and so on. In every such calculation the overriding consideration must be to gain maximum advantage, regardless of whether that is achieved by helping yourself or hampering the opposition.

Moving on the mat

There is also a non-tactical side to the effective use of the mat. You are at liberty to bowl off the back or the front of it, or off either side – always with the proviso that you do not foot-fault by having both feet outside the confines of the mat at the moment of delivery. In theory, moving forward or backward on the mat will affect length by a foot or so, and you can use that fact to adjust length accordingly. This must be viewed as a desperate remedy for unmanageable length, since it is only by bowling from the one position that you will be able to hold line. To disrupt line for a mere foot of length is hardly sensible. And if you bowl from the back of the mat you will find yourself grounding the bowl dangerously near the front edge.

THE TACTICAL GAME

INDOOR AND ARTIFICIAL OUTDOOR SURFACES

The popularity of the indoor game has been growing apace for years now, and will continue to do so. This is partly in response to television exposure of this variety of the game, partly a comment on the decline in quality of outdoor greens.

There can be no question that indoor greens provide a truer test of pure bowling skill than outdoor greens possibly can, because of the near-uniformity of conditions. This is not to say that such bowling provides better sport, let alone a more enjoyable experience. Nothing can be better than bowling on a well-kept green on a perfect summer's day with the sun on your back and maybe just the occasional gentle breeze to fan your face. This prospect of paradise does not feature in the indoor game, but neither does the threat of bowling hell.

The indoor carpet is laid on a concrete screed, with an interposing underlay. They are pretty nearly always true, although they vary a little in pace. Therefore they must be read during the trial ends, and it is a big mistake to waste any trial bowls. Also, although to nothing like the same extent as an

The proliferation of excellent indoor facilities has played an important role in popularising the sport.

The portable rink used for the World Indoor Championship arrives at Preston Guildhall in sections. The sections are slotted together and the carpet rolled out to make a seamless – and quite excellent – surface.

THE TACTICAL GAME

outdoor green, carpets can be affected by climatic conditions. They run a little quicker on a dry frosty morning than on a sticky day.

If you are in a position to do so you will enjoy the best of both worlds by bowling outdoors during the season, and then move to an indoor rink for the winter months. The transition from one to the other is more difficult in spring than it is in autumn. There is a world of difference between the quickish, billiard-table-smooth indoor surface and the outdoor green on opening day, which is likely to be heavy with winter rain, under-rolled and under-cut. It can seem to take a mighty effort just to reach a long jack, and women in particular often struggle to reach. It is important to get your body weight right over the bowl, so as to achieve the required strength of shot without having to rely on excessive arm swing. And coping all of a sudden with surface irregularities (most pronounced after a winter's neglect) may test your temper as much as your skill. By comparison, moving indoors at the end of the season, when the outdoor green has had a full season's play and maintenance, is much less of a shock to the system. Reining back a little on weight (and adjusting to the truer surface) is easy enough.

The outdoor carpet

A more recent development is the synthetic outdoor green, similar to artificial grass tennis courts. When prototypes appeared several years ago they excited considerable interest, because they promised true running under outdoor conditions. While they delivered this, to a large extent, they were adjudged a failure because of seemingly-intractable drainage problems. Manufacturers have persisted in their endeavours, however, and recent results are very promising. The artificial green, with its considerable maintenance advantages, may be a pointer to the future for the outdoor game. Outdoor carpets are particularly important in the development of the game in Spain.

After initial teething troubles, outdoor artificial greens are beginning to show great promise. In particular, they may be instrumental in spreading the game to countries without a bowls tradition, as this Spanish example indicates.

83

SHOT SELECTION

This subject could make a complete book in itself, and even then the topic would not be exhausted. Choice of shot is, after all, the only cerebral aspect of the game. Every head is unique, and as it takes shape it poses challenges the like of which you have never quite seen previously. In a sense, every end presents you with a series of one-off problems to solve. What you have to do is apply your powers of observation, draw on your experience and exercise your judgment, all in tandem.

This sounds a tall order, and shrewd shot selection is certainly that. There is the objective state of the head as your first consideration, and the condition of the green as it affects your options. Then there is the matter of your bowling skills, how your strengths or weaknesses reflect realistically on the options, restricting or extending them. And then there is your perception of your opponent's strengths and weaknesses. The list has just begun. What are your chances of making the shot? What is the potential profit in its success, the potential loss in its failure? And profit and loss may not be just a simple matter of shots scored either way. The state of the match might be such that risking big loss for equivalent gain is quite in order – or quite daft!

The bewildering complexity of the calculations surrounding shot selection should not lead to despair. There are general principles to guide you, which are universal in their applicability even if they must be adapted to the particular circumstances. As an obvious example, some considerations are more relevant to team play than to singles, and that will be fully explored in the following chapter. For now, the discussion is intended to be general, and from the examples given it will be apparent if solo or team play is implied.

Percentage play

The term 'playing the percentage shot' is frequently misunderstood when it is applied to the choice of shot in any game of skill. It has a dull, defensive ring to it, and can be made to sound like the refuge of the timorous. This badly mis-

David Corkhill of Ireland stares intently at a close head, weighing the odds.

THE TACTICAL GAME

construes what is in fact the fundamental truth of all tactical play. The percentage shot is in itself neither defensive nor offensive, neither timid nor bold. It is the shot suggested by the cool appraisal of all relevant factors as being most appropriate to the circumstances. That appraisal starts by acknowledging the various plausible options and then weighing them up against each other (it goes without saying that if there is only one realistic option then it is, by default, the percentage shot). Perhaps shot A is at first glance the favourite. That may be because it is the easiest of several positive shots to execute, or because, though difficult, it will, if successful, result in a big count, or because whatever, it makes no difference. Shot A has the most superficial attraction.

Weighing the odds

Now consider the following, in logical sequence. How likely are you to make the shot? What do you gain if you make it? What do you risk losing if you miss it? Is there a secondary position if you just miss, or is it neck-or-nothing? In other words, taking into account all plausible outcomes, does the prospect of success outweigh the risk of failure? Whether the answer is yes or no, you have not finished with your calculations. Consider shots B and C. How do they stand up to the same scrutiny? All in all, which of the shots under consideration truly satisfies the criterion of being the best gamble under the circumstances? They may all be very good gambles, but which is best? They may all reflect the desperate nature of your plight, but which is the least awful gamble? Whatever emerges from that calculation is the percentage shot. It may be the shot with the highest risk of failure (because if it succeeds it may win you the match and if it fails you will still remain comfortably ahead), or it may be the most cautious of the bunch (because failure would put you out of the match and success would not be similarly dramatic). In any case that is the percentage shot, calculated to the best of your bowling brain.

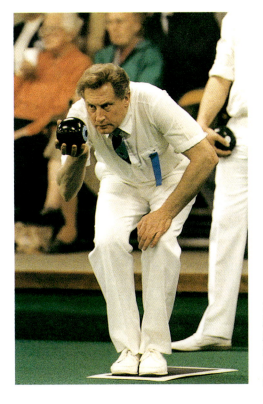

The player pictured has clearly selected his shot before coming to the mat, and is now, correctly, focused entirely on his shot.

Just because it is the percentage shot is of course no guarantee of success, but even failure does not alter its status as the percentage shot. And by the flip side of the coin, a non-percentage shot that comes off remains a non-percentage shot. In other words, the percentage shot is what it is, whether you choose to play it or not, regardless of outcome. It is an inexorable rule that good percentage players tend to succeed more than do those who consistently flout the odds, but that does not mean you should become a slave to percentages. Sometimes a shot against the odds will succeed dramatically, and who is then to say it was the wrong choice of shot? It may be that you just felt the gods were with you, and such a feeling is not to be despised as a factor in your calculations. All good players take

BOWL TO WIN

Will it reach? There is of course no guaranteed result when you play the percentage shot, but the player who most correctly assesses and consistently plays the percentage shot is likely to prevail.

genuine risks from time to time, but the point remains that you will never achieve consistent results if you ignore the realities of percentage play.

Experience alone can provide you with a sound basis for shot selection, but there are guidelines that should apply to novice and expert alike. During the trial ends, when you are trying to establish line and length, you will notice if the green is two-paced. If it is, decide which side suits you better, and try to stick to it where possible, forehand one way, backhand the other. As the head develops there will be situations in which you must play the 'wrong' hand, and you should not hesitate to do so, but as soon as possible revert to your favourite. You want to settle into the groove of a rhythmical line and length. This again reinforces the point about striving for equal confidence on your forehand and backhand deliveries.

Remember that length is more difficult to achieve than line, and because the green (outdoors) tends to quicken

during the first few ends you should try to get into the drawing groove immediately, so that you can respond to subtle changes in length. This means that you should be sparing with the heavy shots early on, because they are of no help in establishing length. This is particularly the case in the team game, if you are playing down the order. The lead and second will be gaining drawing experience from the outset, but if you are skipping you could find yourself relying on takeout shots from the very beginning. Where does that leave you if, a few ends in, you are suddenly faced with a draw to an open jack? How on earth can you achieve that, even if you have a real sitter with feet to spare, if you are completely out of touch with the pace of the green? Never, under any circumstances, allow yourself to lose touch with the pace of the green.

Close may not be good enough
When you are drawing to the jack, close looks good, but not all close is equally good. Just behind or just in front is ideal, but jack high and just to the side is a poor result. The jack-high bowl is perfectly placed for a rest shot, and, if it escapes that fate it is still going to be left high and dry by a trail.

It is wise to work on the assumption that it is by winning the majority of close ends that you are most likely to win the game. So develop the habit of keeping things tight from the outset. If you are fortunate to get away to a flying start, by all means press home your advantage, but do not risk squandering that precious lead to do so. The only real exception to this policy is where you are streets ahead and a big count will get you past the winning post. In such circumstances you are likely to be feeling both aggressive and confident, and it would be mean advice to suggest you throttle back and coast home. You are supposed to gain enjoyment as well as victory. Just bear in mind, however, that every once in a while you will come a cropper (as the authors have done) and see that unassailable lead disappear like a mirage.

In a match played over a specified number of ends you really should do everything possible to curb the reckless impulse, however much it may go against the grain. If there is a golden rule for the chancy shot it is this. During the first two-thirds of a match, look for the opportunity to make a big count because if it comes off it will put you in the driving seat. Pull it off twice and you may romp home. During the last third of the match, if you are winning, do nothing to jeopardise your position. The pressure is on your opponent, and you should tighten it ruthlessly. If you are losing, look to claw your way back bit by bit, rather than gamble on a dramatic counterstrike, although of course that principle must be abandoned if you are running out of ends.

Another point to consider is damage limitation. While you set off to win every end, you will frequently find yourself in a position later on where your cause is pretty conclusively lost. Admittedly, any end can be saved with a perfect shot, but assume for the moment that miracles are in short supply and that you are going to lose the end. How should you go about fighting a rearguard action? If you are three down and have a good chance to make it one down, that would seem the prudent thing to do. But what if missing the shot might set you even further back, by taking out your best bowl, for instance?

As a general policy, decline any shot which, if it fails, will leave you worse off than you were. Even the chance of taking shot with a perfect delivery is not worth the risk of turning a two-shot deficit into a four-shot deficit. This cannot be a hard and fast rule. If those two shots are all your opponent needs to win the game, then you must risk all.

BOWL TO WIN

1 Assume that this situation has cropped up in the early stages of a singles game. While red holds shot, the head is clearly against him in the sense that any further activity there is likely to result in loss rather than gain. Both forehand and backhand are pretty congested, and it would need a very accurate bowl to squeeze through for a second. The prospect of failure outweighs the possibility of success, which would suggest that red should decline his last bowl.

However, since it is early on, red would be better advised to seize the opportunity for a little purposeful practice. He could bowl out by the strings, either on the forehand or backhand, whichever he is more curious to experience. By aiming, say, for a spot near the ditch, he would get a useful feeling for both line and length to an area he might really need to bowl to in the very next end. Alternatively, he could try for the centreline – taking care to stay well short of that treacherous head! The general point is, do not omit to play a bowl unless you are certain that it would be a complete waste of effort to do so.

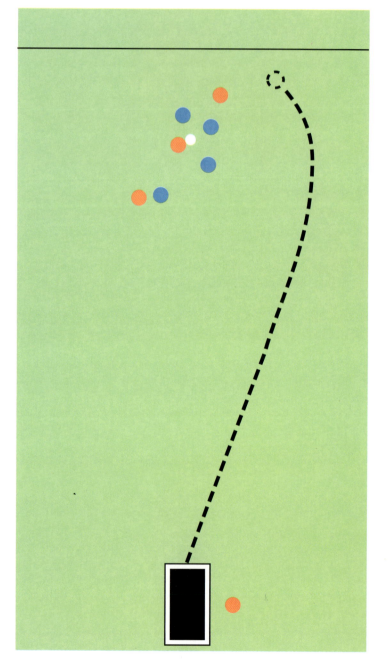

THE TACTICAL GAME

2 The perfect shot here would be a tap and lie on blue's shot bowl delivered on the backhand, which would spring the jack towards blue's two back bowls for a count of 3, and quite likely 4. It is, however, probably safer for blue to imagine this shot as a draw, making certain to reach. That way, if the confident, reaching draw does manage to turn the shot bowl over, the reward will still be that 3 or 4-shot score. If it just fails, it should still be near enough to count a second.

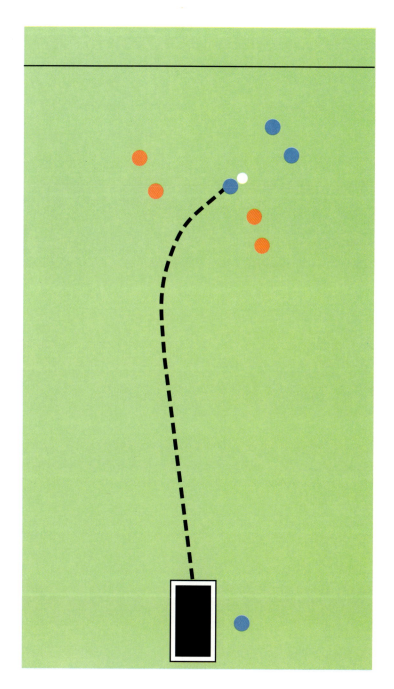

BOWL TO WIN

3 His two short bowls have left blue with a bit of a mountain to climb. With 4 shots against, what is the best way of redressing the situation, or at least minimising the damage? His two short bowls pretty effectively rule out a draw into the head, although it might be just about possible to squeeze one through on the forehand. Realistically, a weighted bowl is required, the choice being between a firm wood and a firing shot.

Unless blue is very confident of his driving ability he should resist the temptation to let fly, in the hope that carnage in the head will solve his problems and maybe, with luck, even yield a winning position. Of course it might happen, but it is possible that the shot will be missed. It would be better, except for the expert driver, to settle for a firm wood, played with minimum ditch weight. It is of vital importance to shake up that head, and while a firm wood will not wreak the havoc of a well-aimed drive, it can only improve blue's position, and it is in the circumstances the percentage shot. And for that shot, blue's two short bowls become of real use. They act like goalposts, beckoning in his bowl. While it would be just possible to go through the 'posts' on the backhand and miss the shot bowl, it is highly unlikely. Since the firm wood will be affected to some extent by bias, all blue has to do is play between the 'posts', either forehand or backhand, whichever is the better hand, and that 4-shot deficit will be reduced, perhaps substantially.

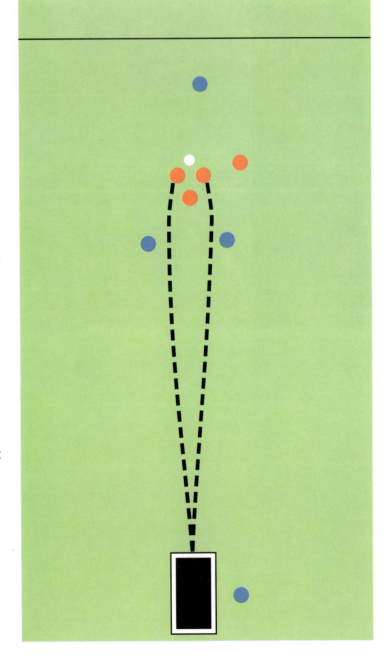

THE TACTICAL GAME

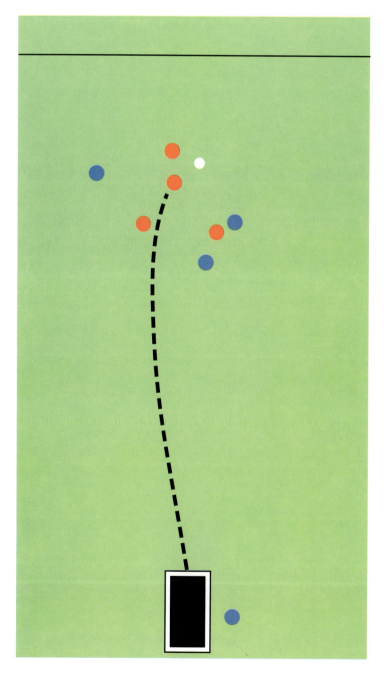

4 Under normal circumstances the forehand draw would be the obvious choice of shot, giving blue every chance of reducing or wiping out the deficit (red lies 2, measure for 3). However, blue knows that the forehand side of the rink in this direction is behaving awkwardly. If he bowls it a little wide it will stick, a little narrow and it will cut across the head. In other words, while a perfect draw is possible, there is little or no margin for error. The obvious is therefore not the percentage shot, because the playing characteristics of the green are just as significant a factor in calculating the percentage shot as is the technical difficulty of the delivery itself, viewed in isolation.

Under these circumstances the better shot is a weighted bowl on the backhand into the head, with the object of breaking up red's position, or trailing the jack to the ditch, or both. Blue's target is large, extending from the red bowl on the left to the jack. He can use as much controlled weight as he feels comfortable with. If he is a confident driver then he should let fly.

These sort of situations frequently occur in competition, when to the spectator the choice of shot seems eccentric, but to the player, who is in possession of superior knowledge (he knows the state of the rink), it is not eccentric at all.

BOWL TO WIN

5 With his third bowl, blue has signalled his intentions: he has driven and missed, winding up on the bank. Red must assume that with his final bowl blue will repeat the exercise, and not necessarily with the same barren result. Therefore he should resist the temptation to draw a third shot. If he does draw successfully, say jack high or thereabouts and a little to the side, all he will have done is present blue with a larger target for a destructive firing shot.

This is the perfect opportunity for a block shot, either forehand or backhand, dead on the centreline. If he can do that it will be a devastating blow, leaving blue pretty conclusively dead in the water. If red fails with the blocker, he has at least done no harm (he has not increased the size of blue's target), and even a 'wasted' short bowl may have an influence by drawing blue's eye during his delivery.

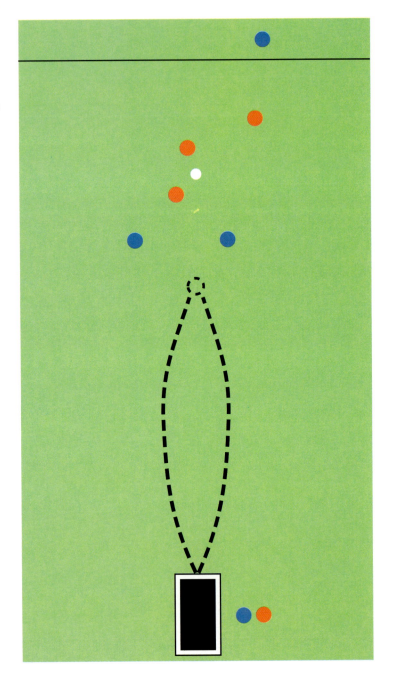

THE TACTICAL GAME

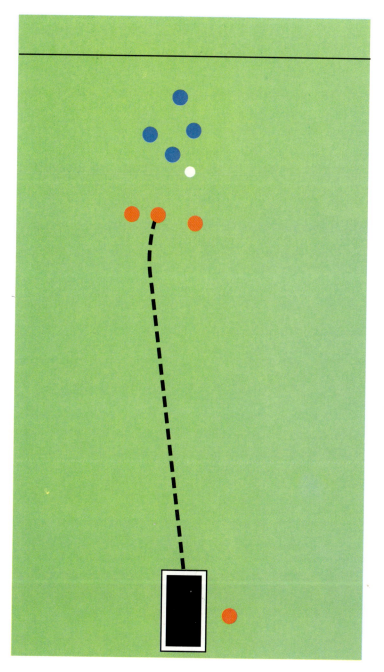

6 Red is in serious trouble here as he comes to deliver his final bowl, facing a count of 3. It frequently happens that critical judgment breaks down under precisely the circumstances that most demand it. Red has played his first three shots on the backhand, and all have fallen short by a couple of feet or so. All he has succeeded in doing is to block himself out of the head on his backhand. So why not draw on the forehand, which is perfectly open?

Wrong! The reason red has been playing on the backhand is that it is his preferred hand on this stretch of green. His deliveries have been consistently under strength, but his line is not bad. On the forehand, by contrast, he would be entering uncharted waters. Assuming this is an outdoor rink, the conditions down that forehand might easily have changed since last he bowled it (if indeed he has, from that mat position and length of jack). It would be a desperately risky move to play that theoretically straightforward forehand.

Red should therefore persist with the backhand, with a yard or so of weight so as to promote one of his three short bowls. They present a large target, and if he can connect with any of them, not a difficult feat, he may get a result, either cutting the deficit to a single or maybe even taking shot.

BOWL TO WIN

7 Red is 2 down as he comes to the mat for his final delivery. The forehand is congested, and the backhand is running noticeably straight, so that an attempted backhand draw would finish wide. Is there anything for it but to let fly and hope for carnage?

Most definitely. Red could try to promote his central bowl with a tap and lie shot, and if he could play that with just a little more weight he might follow through to take 2 shots. That, however, is the counsel of perfection. It would be all too easy to miss the shot. The percentage shot on offer is the run-through, played with at least two yards of running. If red connects with any of the central bowls (a huge target) with enough weight to take it well beyond the jack, his own bowl should follow through to take shot position. The worst scenario is that red hits a blue bowl straight onto the jack for a trail, but that would be bad luck, and in any case would cut the deficit from 2 to 1.

The important thing to remember is that the shot must be played with enough running to take the target bowl well behind the jack, so that it is out of contention. That is the feature of the shot that allows red to be unspecific in his choice of target bowl, thereby giving himself such a large target.

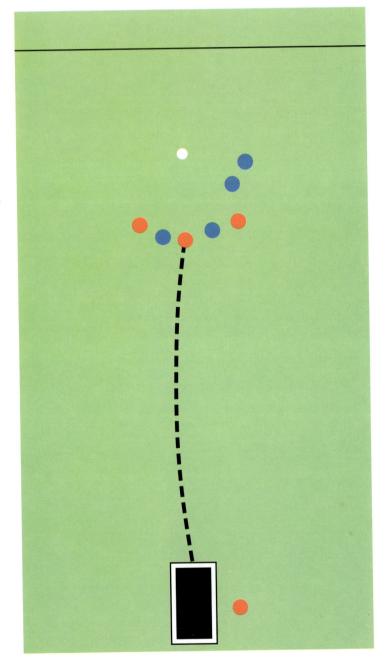

THE TACTICAL GAME

8 Blue is 2 down, and he has no direct path to the jack because the backhand is blocked and the forehand is running too straight to bring the bowl round at the end. The only realistic choice is a wick, even though it is one of the most difficult of all shots. If blue can make contact with the inside of his bowl on the right, with just a little over draw weight, it should bring him nicely onto the jack, maybe even for a gentle trail. If, perchance, he should hit the outside of his target bowl instead, he might propel it in the direction of the jack, although his opponent might with justification consider that a fluke result.

The important thing to remember in this situation is not to play with too much weight. If blue were to hit his own bowl straight on with any serious weight he would knock it out of the head and then run through, thereby losing the end by 3 shots rather than 2.

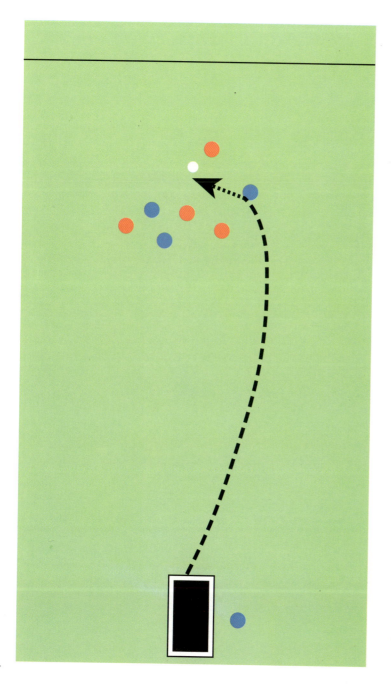

BOWL TO WIN

9 Red is in an enviable position, holding shot and presented with a glorious opportunity to trail the jack for a count of 4. There are two schools of thought, or more accurately, preferences, for taking on this sort of shot. Some bowlers like to imagine that they are drawing to the jack with a little added weight. Others find it more satisfactory to imagine they are drawing to the spot where they would like the bowl to finish, after it has trailed the jack. Either is perfectly acceptable.

There is an added bonus for red here in that his shot bowl prevents the possibility of slicing the jack towards the opponent's bowls. This is often a critical consideration (see following example), because the jack is such a small target that even for the most skilful bowler there is every chance of clipping it on the wrong side, with disastrous consequences. But not here.

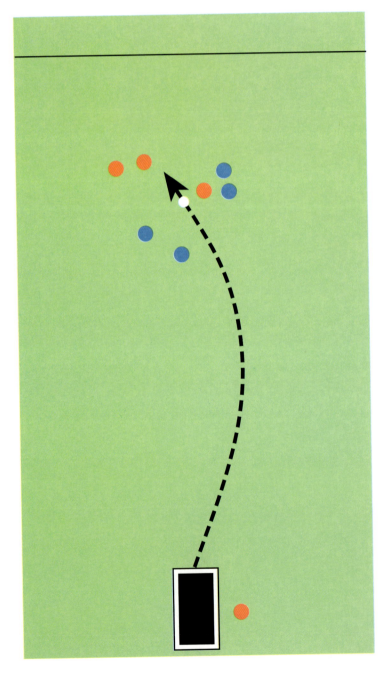

THE TACTICAL GAME

10 This is identical to the previous example, but two bowls earlier, when red does not have that shot bowl preventing an inadvertent slice on the jack. There is a temptation to think that a trail shot is bound to take the jack in the direction the bowl is travelling upon impact, in this case the forehand trail taking the jack towards red's bowls. Not so. Only a fractional error in line can bring the bowl across the face of the jack, with the resultant slice.

This does not mean that red should decline the shot, but he should be very careful not to take too narrow a line. He should approach the jack with a little more than draw weight, conscious that he must err, if at all, on the outside. That way, if he misses the jack he will be in a strong position for his final shot (as in the previous example).

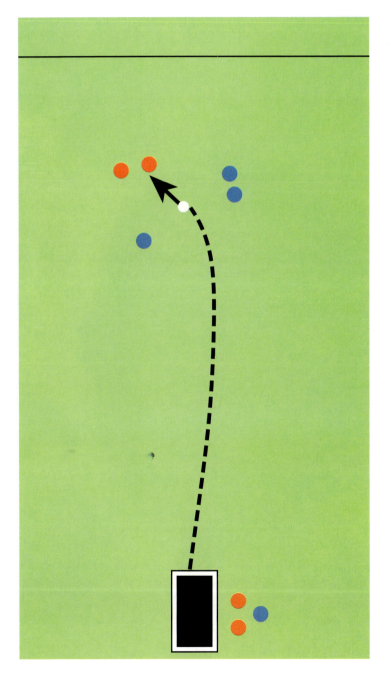

BOWL TO WIN

11 Red has only one realistic shot here: to attempt to spring the jack. The problem is blue's front blocker, which makes it impossible for red to drive at the target bowl (blue's second counter). This means red must play a firm wood, to skim past the blocker but still work with enough bias to swing in on the target. If he succeeds, red will spring the jack out to the right – all the way to the edge of the rink to kill the end, if he is lucky. If he misses the target, either because he has given the blocker too wide a berth or because he has played with too much weight to allow the bias to take sufficient effect, he may well take out his own back bowl, but that is of no great significance because it does not increase the deficit of 2 shots.

An alternative would be to play a forehand draw which, if it were inch-perfect, might reduce the deficit to 1. But even top bowlers can hardly consider the inch-perfect draw the percentage shot when there is an alternative which, though difficult, provides at least a slight margin of error.

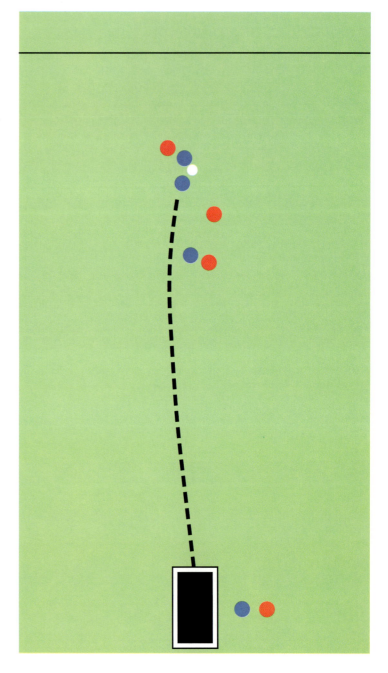

THE TACTICAL GAME

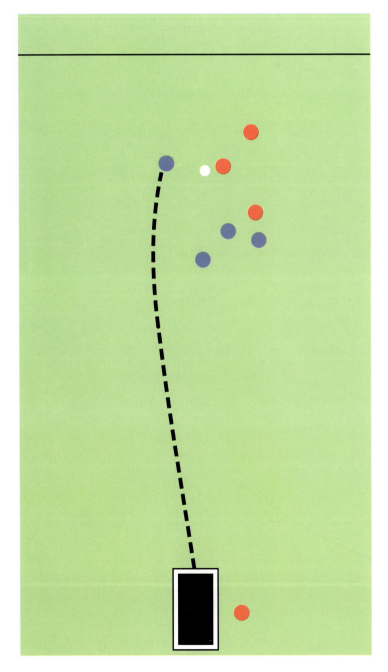

12 Red is lying 1 shot, and depending upon his choice, he can attempt to win the end by 2, 3 or even 4 shots. The easiest alternative is to draw for 2, but that would be a rather unambitious approach. Better to try to remove the offending blue bowl which is lying second shot. Red can do this in one of two ways. He can play with enough weight to clear blue well out of the way. If he does that and runs through himself he lies 3. If he makes full enough contact on blue he may might stay for 4. Or, if he is really feeling confident, he can play positively for the latter result by playing a tap and lie. If he pulls it off he is guaranteed the 4 shots.

The factors that come into play are red's skills and his feeling for the shot. A drive with controlled weight is easier to achieve than the subtle tap and lie. And there is still the chance of making 4 anyway, if the contact is full. Either way red risks little, because he lies shot regardless. He risks only the extra shot he might have gained with the 'safe' draw. But if he can make 3, or better yet 4, this may have a demoralising effect on his opponent. That is a relevant factor in working out the percentage shot (maximum reward for minimum risk), and it is why the easier draw shot should be declined.

BOWL TO WIN

13 There is a marvellous opportunity for red to turn a 2-shot deficit into a 4-shot advantage. All he has to do is drive the jack into the ditch. Not only is the potential gain immense, the risk is negligible. In the worst case scenario he might strike one of blue's front bowls a glancing blow and deflect it into the head, to go 3 down, but that really would be unlucky. Any decent contact on one of those bowls would scatter it, and maybe another blue bowl with it. So the choice is clear. Either a forehand or backhand drive, whichever hand feels most comfortable, with whatever weight (so long as it is ditch weight) red feels most able to control. Success here could be a match-winning blow – in itself, or in its psychological effect on blue.

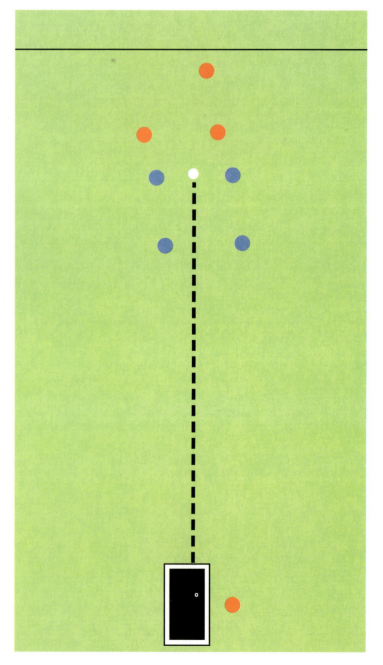

THE TACTICAL GAME

14 Red is 4 shots down, but he is not short of opportunities to redress the balance. To begin with, a perfect draw on either hand would save the day. Consider the forehand draw first. Only a perfect draw would be rewarded with shot, although anything pretty close would cut the deficit to 1. Now if the forehand is red's preferred choice (ie if it is the hand he has been playing throughout the match in this direction, and he has certainly been playing it this end), then the forehand option cannot be ruled out.

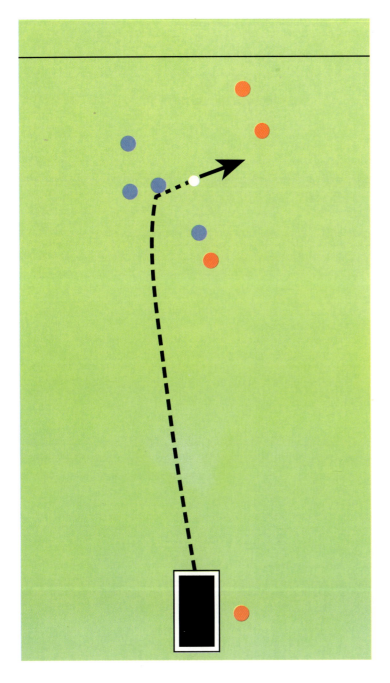

Of more interest objectively, however, is the position on the backhand. Again the perfect draw would be rewarded with shot. However, consider the possibilities of playing into the head with a couple of feet of running – making certain not to take a tight line, which would run the risk of cutting across the front of the jack, thereby leaving him 4 down. If red comes in wide and connects with blue's bowl on the left he is likely either to replace that bowl and cut his deficit to 1 (if he connects full on blue, or, better, on blue's right side), or he may take out the blue bowl and run through out of position, leaving himself 3 down. A bad result would be to clip blue on the left, which would leave the situation unchanged. Therefore, he must aim to be inside that outer blue bowl.

If he does get inside and makes contact with blue's shot bowl, again with a little running, red may gain shot (if he makes contact pretty flush), and if he clips blue on the left side he will be either 2 or 3 down.

If red makes contact with the blue shot bowl's right side and then connects with the jack, however, the situation improves dramatically.

If the jack springs across at right angles red should score 2, but if it springs forward he should be looking at 3 – a wonderful turn of events. Similarly, if he is a little inside that line and trails the jack, 3 again should be the reward. The only possible danger with the trail is that if red plays with a little too much weight he might conceivably drive the jack onto his own back bowl and watch it rebound towards blue's bowls. This is a remote danger.

Therefore, the option of the forehand draw must be weighed against the really exciting possibility of making a big count on the backhand. The most important thing to remember about this backhand is that while precise weight is not critical, it is absolutely imperative to reach.

BOWL TO WIN

15 Blue is to bowl his last, in an end that has started badly and got progressively worse. He is 3 down, and almost certain to go 4 down if he does not do something useful at this final attempt. His best choice might appear to be a draw on the backhand, where a perfect line and length would give him shot. The trouble is, even though he has been playing on the backhand, he has signally failed so far to get close. Does he feel confident of getting it right this time? Even nearly right, of course, would reduce the deficit to 2 or 1.

Blue might consider switching to the forehand, where an accurate bowl with draw weight would reduce his arrears to 1. Or he could play the same shot with a yard of running, and if he gets it right, trail the jack towards his own bowls. That would be a terrific outcome, but is it realistic to come 'cold' to the forehand and expect such accuracy? Perhaps more realistically, blue could play a firm wood at red's second shot, which might just spring the jack in the desired direction. Or he could drive at red's short bowl, which should shake up the head, and might move the jack.

A generation ago, the prevailing wisdom would have been for a saving draw, on the backhand, assuming it is behaving well. Today, on the other hand, there is much less prejudice against the drive. Under the circumstances the best advice would be to disturb the head, either with a weighted bowl, attempting to spring the jack, or a full-blooded drive, attempting at all costs to get rid of some or all of those red bowls.

THE TACTICAL GAME

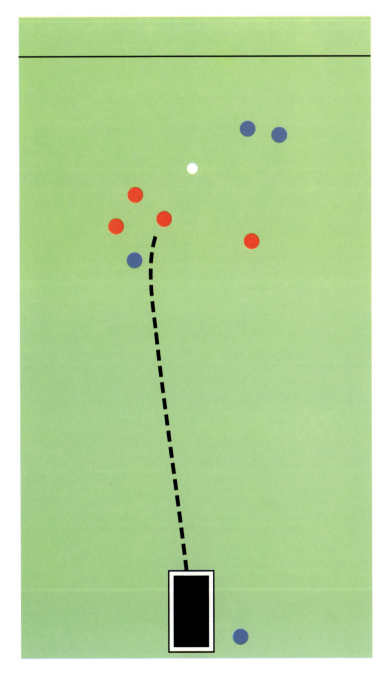

16 Red lies 2 as blue surveys the scene for his final delivery. There is a straightforward draw opportunity on the forehand, although he must be careful to avoid red's front bowl. There is also the possibility of playing for the jack with a little running, aiming to come across the face of the jack and slice it towards blue's two back bowls. This would be a hugely satisfying shot to achieve, but what are the odds of doing so? If missed, it is a wasted bowl.

The backhand holds intriguing possibilities. If blue can play a weighted shot and make full contact with his front bowl he will split the red bowls, and if the gods are smiling he might run through to trail the jack for 3. With the bowls so placed that is a distinct possibility, although not to be counted upon. However, the target on the backhand is wide, and any weighted bowl that gets well in amongst that head is likely to improve blue's situation. For example, if he misses his own target bowl but connects with the red bowl to the right, he will at least clear out one of red's counters and might easily run through to take shot.

In every such situation, the behaviour of the rink and the player's preferred hand are large considerations in working out the percentage shot. Here they are probably decisive, since objectively there is little to choose between the prudent forehand draw and the bold backhand looking for a count.

BOWL TO WIN

17 The point of this example is not the choice of shot, which is obvious, but in the danger lurking. While red could use his final bowl to draw shot, that would be timid in the extreme. The shot to play is the trail to the ditch, for a count of 4. But beware! The forehand to the jack may look innocuous enough, but there is potential peril. If red takes too much green and makes contact with blue's shot bowl, he will go down by the maximum 4 which it was his intention to score.

This is more than a theoretical danger. Allcock has drawn it from memory, having once witnessed a club final where red was leading 17-14 and played the trail to end the game. He came in wide and struck blue, with the result described. So instead of finishing the game with a flourish he was suddenly 17-18. So shaken was he that he did not score again, to go down 17-21.

The moral of this cautionary tale is not to avoid taking opportunities, and this is a real one, but never to lose sight of potential danger in the flush of enthusiasm. As long as you are mindful of the potential pitfall here, and therefore make certain not to come in wide, then the trail is an exciting opportunity to be seized.

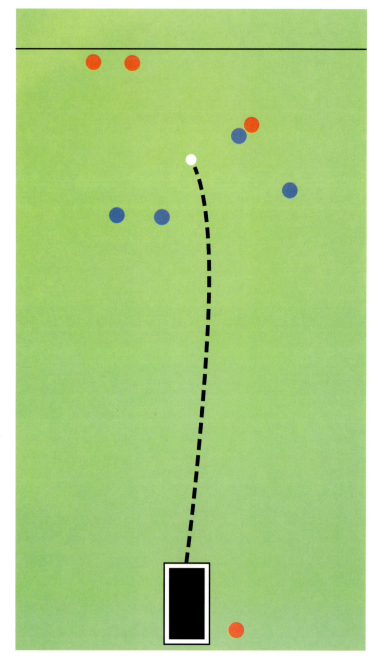

THE TACTICAL GAME

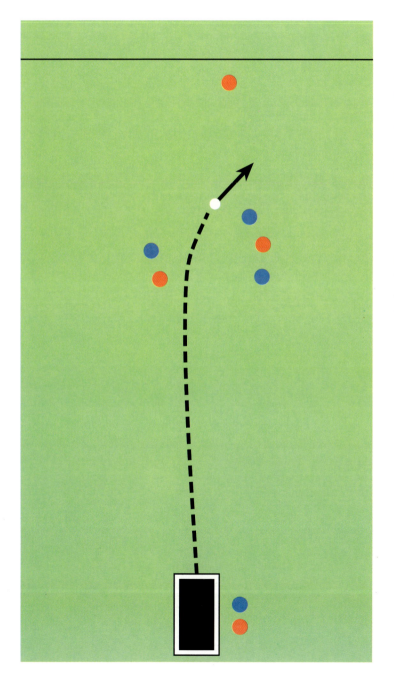

18 Imagine blue is leading 20-19 and red has the final bowl. Although he is lying shot, and needs only the single for the game, blue is in serious trouble. He can play the draw, either forehand or backhand, but the danger lies in red's excellent back bowl. Drawing a second shot would simply mean increasing the size of red's target as he set out to drive the jack to the ditch and follow it in for 2 shots and the game.

In theory, blue could try to improve on red's back bowl, but so good is red's position that blue would have to draw literally to the brink of the ditch – something no one can have confidence in achieving. A perfect blocker could make things difficult for red, but he would still be able to reach blue's shot bowl with controlled weight and score the necessary 2. Blue may well view this as a 'Catch 22 situation', but there is an escape route. If he can trail the jack to a less exposed position, say well behind that cluster on the right, red would need a lucky break to ditch it, and blue would end the match with his single.

BOWL TO WIN

19 This example illustrates a principle that is easily overlooked, even at the upper levels of the game. Blue has a full house, and red has a final chance to do something about it. With the jack in the ditch, the only way red can win the end is by out-drawing blue's shot bowl. If he can do that, well and good. But if he overbowls slightly and winds up in the ditch, he has lost 4 shots. Obviously, if blue needs only a single for the game, then red has no choice but to go for it. But if red is not facing oblivion, it is by far the better course of action to draw for second shot (easy here), and let blue have his single. Knowing when to give a shot is just as important as knowing when to take one.

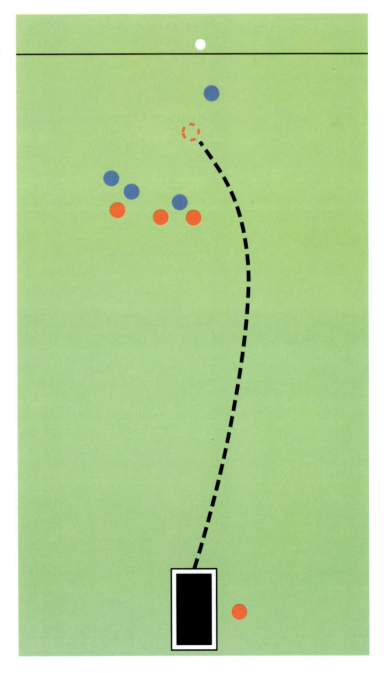

THE TACTICAL GAME

20 This is an actual shot played by Tony Allcock at a critical juncture of an important match. It was during the singles semi-finals at Preston Guildhall during the 1992 World Indoors Championship. Allcock's opponent was the Australian Ian Schuback, and Schuback was leading 5-3 in the final set.

As Allcock recalls: 'The prospect was not pleasing, but it wasn't hopeless either. Ian's short bowl, about 3 feet short of the jack, ruled out the forehand, but there was room for manoeuvre on the backhand. Ian's shot bowl was jack high and about 6 inches away. I held second and third shots.

'From where I was standing on the mat I could not see the jack, but I had a clear view of Ian's shot bowl. I calculated that if I could take his bowl a couple of feet through the head, I could make a count of 3, and take the lead at this vital stage. My chief worry was the portable rink itself, which was tending to swing hard on the backhand. This meant that if I was at all narrow I might make a disastrous contact with his front bowl, promote it, and give Ian the 2 he needed for the match. So I took plenty of green and played the shot.

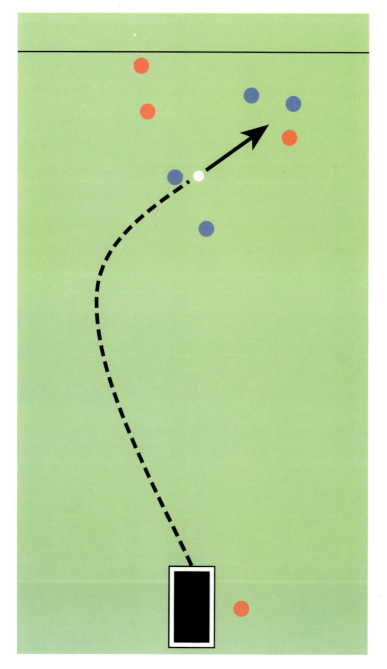

'As soon as it left my hand it looked good, and I chased it up the green in my excitement. Even late in the shot I was anxious that I might have erred slightly by going wide, and until very near the end there seemed a possibility of sliding by on the outside, but I was counting on that final swing to bring me flush onto the target. The swing, when it came, brought horror to my face. My bowl swung right across the face of Ian's bowl, and sprung the jack straight to his two back bowls. A few seconds later we were shaking hands, and my hopes of another singles title were dashed.

'In the interview room I was asked about the shot, and I said that under identical circumstances I would play it again, only this time I might get the intended result. It was a risky shot, and maybe I was a little unlucky, but at the highest levels of competition an inch or so either way can decide matches. In this case those finest of margins brought me disaster, but often enough they have brought me triumph.'

BOWL TO WIN

21 This shot is one of the most memorable in the history of the game. It is played by David Bryant during the singles final of the World Championships, in 1988, in New Zealand.

Bryant and his good friend Willie Wood were level on 22-all (the match was 25-up) when rain interrupted play. After sitting in the pavilion for an hour and a half they walked out to resume battle. Bryant remarked to Wood, as they made their way down the rink, that here they were, having cooled their heels for such a long time, in a situation where it could all be over in a single end. But, Bryant points out, 'I never for a moment thought it would really happen that way.'

What did happen is etched on his memory. 'We had a trial end in each direction, which Willie bowled slightly better than I did. Then he led off, since he had scored last to make it 22-all. After we had both played twice he was lying 2, with bowls close together and about a yard short of the jack. Mine were both behind the jack, further away. When he drew a third, this time behind, I was getting worried. So I fired at his two front bowls, split them perfectly and could afford a sigh of relief. At least he could not score the 3 needed for the match.

'Willie drew his final bowl in close, to leave the position illustrated as I came to the mat for my final attempt. I had the option of trying to outdraw Willie on either hand, or trying to rest against his shot bowl. However, in the circumstances of the 'new' green I was none too secure on the draw, as my first two attempts showed. Unhesitatingly, I opted again for the firing shot.

'Like my third shot, this one was bang on target. I caught Willie's shot bowl absolutely full, and drove it into the the side of his second bowl. The target bowl then raced through to the ditch, while Willie's second bowl moved off slowly to the right. My own bowl ran through quickly, and clipped the moving bowl on its left side, sending it off to the strings. My bowl stayed on the green. There were only three bowls in play – all of them mine! I flung my arms into the air as I realised that I had won the match. That cannon onto the moving bowl was a freakish result, but it was one of the most decisive shots I have ever played.'

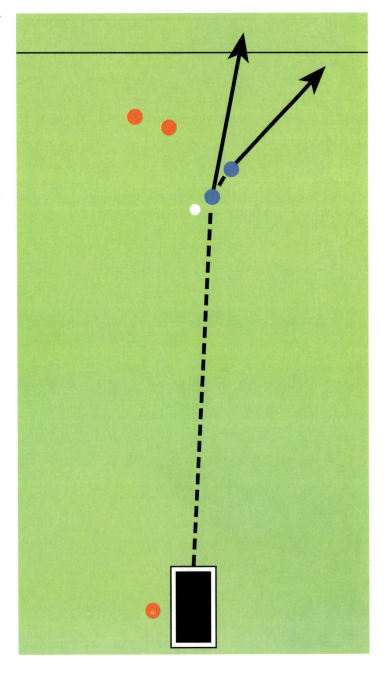

THE TACTICAL GAME

22 In the final of the 1990 World Indoor Pairs Championship, the authors were defending the title against Australians Ian Schuback and Jim Yates. The match was all square at 2 sets all and in the deciding set Allcock and Bryant were trailing 4-6, but lying a single shot with Allcock holding final bowl.

Anything on the forehand was easy to discount, as was the draw on the backhand. The ideal shot was a weighted bowl to ditch the jack, score 3 and win the deciding set. But consider the risks. The Australian best bowl partially obscured the jack, making a drive straight to the jack impossible. So it would have to be a firm wood, using the bias to skirt round the Australian bowl. The danger lay in taking too narrow a line and whipping into the Australian bowl, which would then take out the authors' shot bowl and spell defeat.

An alternative was to decline the bowl and settle for the single, reducing the arrears to 5-6. Allcock recalls: 'We dithered a bit. David was leaning slightly towards the cautious choice – no shot. For my part, I fully appreciated the risks, but believed I could pull off the shot and win the match there and then.

'The percentage shot (or non-shot) could be argued either way, but of course confidence is an important factor in such a calculation. I decided to go for it, and as always my partner was as committed to the shot as I was (whatever his inner reservations). My line with controlled weight was perfect, the jack raced away to the ditch and the title remained ours.'

KEY POINTS
- Reading the green is a vital part of the game
- The faster the green, the more difficult it is to make fine judgments of length
- When there is a sidewind it is usually advisable to bowl into the wind
- Learn to cast the jack accurately
- Tracking is inevitable, and clever use of the mat will enable you to avoid it
- Set long jacks to begin with
- The jack-high bowl is a loser
- Indoor greens need to be read
- Always calculate the percentage shot, even if you then choose not to play it
- Resist the temptation to try to win hopeless ends, and limit the damage

SINGLES, PAIRS AND TEAM PLAY
4

To the uninitiated, the variety of contests described by the term bowls is bewildering. If the situation were like tennis it would be simple – singles and doubles for both sexes, and mixed doubles. And the same rules and scoring system indoors and outdoors, anywhere in the world. This is in stark contrast with the complexities of the bowling world.

Peter Belliss of New Zealand has long been established as one of the world's leading singles players, as well as a supreme bowling stylist.

SINGLES, PAIRS AND TEAM PLAY

To begin with, there are singles competitions indoors and outdoors. In both cases there is a target score, 25-up in any tournament held under the auspices of the World Bowls Board (formerly the International Bowling Board), but 21-up in England, whose English Bowling Association refuses to tamper with its traditional scoring system. This means that there is one scoring system for the World, Commonwealth and British Isles championships, another for the English. And, as every armchair fan knows, an altogether different system for televised bowls, where sets were introduced to heighten the drama. The one thing standard about singles is the number of bowls played, four apiece.

Pairs becomes more complicated. Except for indoor televised bowls, the match is played over 21 ends and the bowlers have four bowls each (making it a 16-bowl game). The televised game repeats the singles set formula, but restricts the bowlers to two bowls apiece. So while the pairs game under all other circumstances is radically different from singles, on television the two are very similar. The televised pairs is in fact tactically identical to singles, with the four bowls on each side shared out.

Taking fours before triples, which is really an odd-ball game, it is exactly the same tactically as (conventional) pairs, with each player having two bowls (ie a 16-bowl game), and it is played over 21 ends. Triples is dismissed by some as a bastard game, with each player holding three bowls, giving the potential for a jam-packed 18-bowl head. To give it rough parity with fours in terms of bowls delivered by each player, triples is restricted to 18 ends.

Then there are the Crown Green and Federation codes, but that is another story....

For club bowlers fours is the most common configuration, maximising the social aspect of the game as well as rink usage.

SINGLES

In bowls as in all games, the head-to-head confrontation of singles provides a special excitement. The gladiatorial nature of such a clash is the stuff of drama, and it is relished by players and spectators alike. It is also the simplest version of the game, because self-reliance is the only possible consideration. You are both lead and skip and so have only to know your own mind, whereas in a pairs or team configuration you are (quite properly) distracted some of the time by thoughts of others. For once, self-centredness is a virtue.

To be a good singles player you have to enjoy the solitary nature of the struggle, the feeling that your destiny is in your hands alone. Victory is a personal triumph, defeat free from recriminations (except self-recrimination). If that does not hold much appeal (and it may not, even if you are keenly competitive), then concentrate your energies on team play, which has its own special rewards.

The complete player

In terms of bowling skills, the successful singles player requires ability across the entire range. He (and of course she, but the authors are reflecting their experience) will probably have a good grounding in every team position, is likely to be a useful skip and is certain to be an excellent lead, even if that is no longer the position played. The reason for singling out the lead and the skip is that the demands of these two positions encompass the singles game. The reason for emphasising the lead is that singles puts a huge premium on drawing ability, the lead's sole function. There is an old saying that in singles the good lead will

Australia's Ian Schuback is on top of the world at his moment of victory to become 1992 World Indoors Singles Champion.

SINGLES, PAIRS AND TEAM PLAY

BOWL TO WIN

The high points are good when you reach them – and here is a summit worth remembering: Tony Allcock having won the World Singles title at Worthing in 1992.

beat the good skip, and while both authors have enjoyed skipping and singles success simultaneously in their careers, they certainly accept the underlying sentiment.

The reason the draw shot is so dominant in singles is that there are only eight bowls in play, which provides nothing like the scope for building up the sort of complicated heads that can be converted by a masterstroke at the very end, to make a huge count. Ones and twos are the order of the day, and the way to pick up those ones and twos is to outdraw your opponent. It is safe to say that the player drawing the better on the day should win the match.

All general tactical considerations apply to singles play. You must get the measure of the green quickly, choose your best hand, sort out line and length to the jack, and get your first bowl there or thereabouts (but never jack high). Treat the first bowl as the most important in every end. If your first bowl gains shot, get your second even closer, preferably on the other side of the jack. One bowl just behind, the other just in front, is ideal. If your opponent has outdrawn your first bowl draw again. It is important to get a second bowl into the head before trying to convert. If you are holding shot after two bowls, you have the upper hand, with your opponent under pressure.

Drawing power wins in the end

As stated earlier, be chary of using heavy shots during the early stages. If your opponent has a fondness for driving himself out of trouble let him get on with it, while you hone line and length. Remember that he is attacking the head because he is under pressure, so do not be intimidated or tempted to do battle with him. Nobody can keep it up accurately forever. If he is temporarily on song with his drives he may win the applause; if you persist with accurate drawing you will win the match.

Keep it tight, being prepared to give one if there is danger. Your opponent cannot get far away on singles. Think carefully before you try a firm wood. It is less accurate than the drive, yet if you miss it you have a bowl out of the head. Make sure you have a back bowl before trying a blocker, and remember that the blocker is a high risk shot, with no secondary value if it fails. Always have at least two bowls in the head before attempting a positional shot.

From his first bowl, watch your opponent with a beady eye, looking for his strengths and weaknesses. Play to his weaknesses as well as your own

SINGLES, PAIRS AND TEAM PLAY

strengths, and try to prevent him from settling into his preferred rhythm. Make imaginative use of mat and jack, to find a winning length for yourself and a losing one for him. Never change a winning length, even if your opponent is bowling well to it too. If you are winning, it must be suiting you better. Identical logic applies to a losing length.

Relentless pressure

The only strategical consideration is to put your opponent under pressure from start to finish. Get an early lead and then pile on the pressure. Because you need a set score to win never let up for a moment. Even the most impressive lead can be thrown away by failure to press home the advantage – all the way to the winning post. Never let up, even if you are leading 20-2. Matches, even at the highest level, have been lost from that position. Once the concentration slips, the rest will surely follow. The term killer instinct may sound excessively violent when applied to such a non-violent game, but it is as relevant to bowls as to boxing.

If you fall behind at the start do not panic. Redouble your efforts and try to get back bit by bit, in ones and twos, rather than risk dropping even further behind by taking on chancy shots. If you start to creep back towards level terms you will have reversed the pressure, and if you overtake your opponent he may become demoralised. Even if you appear hopelessly behind, never surrender. Your opponent may ease up with the winning post in sight, allowing you a chink of daylight. If that happens and you are already resigned to losing, then you are giving it to him on a plate. Make him beat you. And if he does get casual, and you do come back at him, he may panic. It is entirely feasible for a player far in arrears to gain the psychological upper hand and surge to victory. It happens all the time in tennis and snooker, and bowls singles is that type of game.

David Bryant is far and away the most successful singles player in the history of the game.

PAIRS

Pairs is a very satisfying game because it provides comradeship without the burden of man-management, which is an essential element of team play. The authors have enjoyed prolonged success both in singles and as team skips, but in recent years it is as a winning pairs combination that they have so strongly caught the public eye, via the television screen. Like all good partnerships, theirs is based on trust and mutual respect, an unmistakable feature in all their appearances together.

In a sense, Allcock and Bryant make an odd couple. Both are vastly experienced skips, which is the position to which ambitious players normally aspire. At the club level certainly, and even at international level, there is a natural tendency for pairings to be based on complementary qualities. The qualities under consideration are youth and experience, enthusiasm and wisdom, raw talent and cultivated skill. The conventional pairing is therefore the up-and-coming lead with the veteran skip. Quite apart from the obvious potential strength of such a partnership, it has the merit of sidestepping possible rivalry on the rink – a fatal situation if it is allowed to develop. The young lead knows who is in charge and the older skip can help him without feeling

John Price (left) and Stephen Rees of Wales form a long-established and successful pairing.

SINGLES, PAIRS AND TEAM PLAY

any threat to his very well-earned position.

Clearly, despite their disparity in ages, Allcock and Bryant do not fit this mould. Bryant may be the most experienced top-class bowler in the world, and that by a very wide margin, but Allcock is no talented tyro. He was once that, as indeed was Bryant a generation earlier, but their current partnership can hardly be described as a blend of youth and experience. Furthermore, it is the younger man who skips. How did this come about, and why does it work?

To answer the second question first, it works because they feel no rivalry within the partnership. Because neither has anything to prove to the other, either is happy to play lead to the other's skip, and has done so. And if there were the slightest reason for swapping positions, even at this stage, they would not hesitate to do so. That, in fact, is how the present situation came about.

Role reversal

In 1986, they entered the World Indoor Pairs Championship, with Bryant in his familiar skip's role and Allcock happy to lead, because he was in excellent drawing form. In the event, they lost their opening match. Because the competition at that time was conducted on a round robin basis for the preliminary stages, they were still in with a chance, and they decided to swap positions. With Allcock skipping the pair went on to win the title, and that is the way they have played together ever since. By 1994 it had brought them six World Indoor titles.

Their secret is that they stick scrupulously to their roles. Allcock is of course extremely attentive to his partner's advice, but it is always tendered as advice. Despite his incomparable experience, Bryant never by word or gesture attempts to usurp his younger skip's position. For his part, Allcock never ducks his responsibilities as skip just because he is teamed with so formidable a lead.

Another Midland Bank World Indoor Pairs title for the authors. They won the Midland Bank Pairs in 1986, 1987, 1991 and 1992 – and in 1989 and 1990 won the same world title when it was sponsored by Embassy.

ALLCOCK ON BRYANT

David and I first came together on a World Championship stage in 1980, when I played number 2 to his skip in the triples at Melbourne, and we won the title. Four years later we won a silver medal in the World Championships at Aberdeen, this time in the pairs, with me skipping. So by the time we teamed up for the World Indoor Pairs Championship in 1986 we knew each other's games well. I had achieved enough in the game by then not to feel at all intimidated at finding myself in harness with a living legend – not that David has ever intimidated anyone, except his opponents by the sheer brilliance of his play!

'It seemed sensible for me to lead, not for any reasons connected with David's

seniority, but because I had been drawing for some time at the very peak of my ability. In fact I would virtually draw my way to the Singles Championship that year. David had lost none of his appetite for skipping, and who could ask for a better skip? He was master of every shot in the book, a brilliant tactician and an inspirational team leader.

'Because we were dissatisfied with the way we performed in the opening match, we took the rather bold step of switching positions. It worked a treat, and we have never looked back. David has preached all his life about the unique importance of the draw shot, and he practises what he preaches. He is simply an excellent lead.

'Just as I have enormous respect for his playing ability, I find David's personal presence on the green invaluable. Even though I am skip, and must make the big decisions, it is mightily reassuring to be able to draw on his advice. No one can read a head better than David. And he has such a marvellous out-going personality, which is just what I need in a partner because I am, by nature, a more withdrawn sort of character. He never stops encouraging me, as viewers will know. Perhaps they smile too as they hear those inimitable Somerset tones urging my bowl on, willing it to its target – "Come on, Tony! Come on, Tony! Good Shot, Tony!"

'During the 1994 Championship, there was an incident that typified the spirit David brings onto the green. We lost our semifinal match, and while I intend no discredit to our conquerers, the fact is that I got off to a wretched start, and by the time I found my touch we had too much ground to make up.

During those early sets, while I was struggling, and the television commentators were rightly drawing attention to the fact, David never for a moment stopped supporting me on every shot. Good or bad – and they were mostly bad! After one mediocre effort – although I must say that it was a shot that looked worse than it actually was – David remained undaunted. "Good shot, Tony!", rang out to the rafters of the Preston Guildhall. I had to join in the good-natured laughter that came from the spectators, which incidentally had the beneficial effect of relieving the tension I was labouring under. From the television commentary box came the laconic comment to viewers, "Well, there never seems to be a bad bowl for David Bryant..." As a team-mate, that pretty well sums up David Bryant.'

In Allcock's view David Bryant's unswerving loyalty and support are as critical to their successful pairing as is his brilliant talent.

BRYANT ON ALLCOCK

'I started to notice Tony when he was an outstanding junior, and followed his rapid progress through the senior ranks with interest. And by the middle of the 1980s he was winning just about everything in sight. He really had the bowling world at his feet. Unorthodox though that delivery was, it was a model of consistency. He was good on any surface, under any conditions. The draw was, as it should be, the cornerstone of his game. His delicately-weighted shots around the head were a wonder to behold, and if he tended to avoid driving where possible, his accuracy with the rest of his game meant he had little need to fall back on that essentially destructive shot.

'For all these reasons I was – and am – delighted to be paired with him. I was in the autumn of my career, but still keenly competitive, and nothing could have suited me better than to team up with this young star. Although Tony was by this time very experienced at the highest levels of the game, I thought that my much longer experience could still make a valuable contribution.

'As I recall, at the outset of the 1986 World Indoor Championships we tossed a coin for position, since there was no objective reason for deciding. I was happy to skip, but, as it turned out, the switch early on in our roles suited me well. I had been skipping for a very long time, and while I still enjoyed the challenge there is no doubt that the demands of the role over an extended period take a toll. It felt like the most natural thing in the world to pass that mantle to Tony, and I have never regretted it. In fact, I get a positive kick out of leading because trying to perfect the draw shot never ceases to interest me. And it should be remembered that in two-bowl pairs, the lead has every bit as important a role as the skip. Some argue that it is actually the key position, that those opening bowls go more than half way to settling the issue. Whether that is true or not, never make the mistake of thinking that the lead is in any way a warm-up act for the main event to come!

'Tony's greatest strength is his innate natural ability. He always describes himself as an instinctive bowler, by which I think he means that he is not much troubled with theory and just bowls the way that comes naturally to him. That's as may be. His shot-making ability is founded on very sound technique, and as a skip he displays an excellent grasp of tactics. While he has an outstanding record in outdoor bowls, his game is even better suited to the indoor green. The near-perfect conditions of carpet-play reward pure bowling skill, and that is where Tony shines. He makes all those deft little nudge and push shots around the head look easy, and they are anything but that. They require an absolute control of length, and Tony displays that to near-perfection. No one plays a better firm wood, and while it is not his favourite shot, he can play a mean drive when he has to.

'Temperamentally we are well suited. Tony is an intensely focused player, which is a great quality, but I think my relaxed manner helps him loosen up a bit, helps ease the pressure which is always on a skip. I admire the way he copes with the pressure, ice-cool in a crisis, at his most dangerous when the big shot must be played. Tony is of course a great crowd-pleaser, but he's also a bowler's bowler.'

SINGLES, PAIRS AND TEAM PLAY

In Bryant's opinion Tony Allcock's steely nerve reinforces a phenomenal natural ability – making him the perfect partner.

BOWL TO WIN

THE TEAM GAME

Playing with two or three team-mates is very different from pairs, and for many people it is the best way to enjoy bowls. Fours is the particular favourite, and is far and away the most common form of the sport. There are many reasons for this, besides the obvious one of making the most efficient use of a club's facilities. The team game maximises the companionable feature of bowls, and this can be most welcome even for the top players after the stress of singles. Nothing is more enjoyable than being a member of a really close-knit, harmonious team.

Tactically, the team game is utterly fascinating. The harnessing of several individual talents and temperaments to the pursuit of a shared goal is immensely challenging, and to do it successfully is one of the very most rewarding of human activities. To examine how that is done, it is best to analyse the various positions on the team, as they contribute to the team effort.

In this New Zealand tournament razzamatazz reinforces team spirit!

Triumph and dejection. Perhaps the most attractive feature of team play is the fact that such intense emotions can be shared.

SINGLES, PAIRS AND TEAM PLAY

Lead

The authors have been at pains to stress the importance of the draw shot, so it is not surprising that they consider the lead's function utterly critical to team success. They find it surprising that it is so commonly underestimated. The reason, presumably, is that because you have to learn to draw in order to bowl at all, it is the natural starting point for the novice. This is perfectly sound, and it would be a foolish novice who did not see that the lead position was his natural home. However, there is a natural tendency to want to progress down the team order, as though it were a promotion. At club level this is widely encouraged, where a promising lead will not have to wait long for such a 'promotion'. Hence the attitude so often encountered that dismisses the lead as either a beginner or a bowler whose limitations prevent further progress. After all, he only has to throw the jack to the length his skip dictates, and then draw a couple of shots. After that, things get interesting.

The lead directs the marker to centre the jack – which is generally delivered to a length determined by the skip.

This is completely wrongheaded. Setting the length and bowling those first woods is a matter of the utmost importance, as any number 2 can vouch for. There is all the difference in the world between shaping to play into a head with two well-placed draws courtesy of your lead, and looking for a salvage shot to clear up the mess left behind. In every end, one of the number 2s finds himself under pressure to retrieve a disagreeable situation. Like opening batsmen, the lead lays the foundations upon which the remainder of the contest will be built.

A position to hold

If you are a promising lead at club level, and see the wisdom of staying for some time in that position in order to hone your drawing shot, what is your best course of action? Do not allow yourself to be rushed down the order. Instead, try to become such a good lead that a stronger team snaps you up for the same position. Really good leads are like gold-dust, and are likely to make good skips if that is where their ambitions lie. Furthermore, it is often said that the good lead has the most direct route to an international career.

Allcock's early career is a good case in point. In his early 20s, with much junior success behind him, he tried for four successive years to get a place on the England team, either at number 2 or 3. He was not selected. Then for his fifth attempt, in 1978, he decided he would have a better chance of getting chosen as lead. He was chosen, and this became the launching pad for all his subsequent triumphs.

Because the lead only plays the draw shot it is a specialist position (uniquely), and some specialist leads are so good at it, and find its challenges so absorbing, that they never show any interest in moving down the order. John Ottaway of Norfolk has distinguished himself in that position for England for many years, and his team-mates rightly prize his great contribution to their success. They would certainly not like to see him move down the order!

SINGLES, PAIRS AND TEAM PLAY

There are qualities beside drawing ability that mark out the good lead. Because there is a considerable gap between his stints on the mat there is a temptation to switch off when the end is finished, for him. This will not do. For one thing, in a team sport it is important for all members to feel fully involved, at all times. It can be disheartening for players down the order to find the lead retreating into a world of his own while they are in the thick of battle. At a practical level, the lead has plenty to concern himself with. Only by paying keen attention to all the bowls will he be able to detect subtle but significant changes in conditions – tracking, gradual changes in pace, the effects of a stiffening breeze and so forth. He should be constantly engaged in looking for ways to lay ever-better foundations for heads to come.

Shot is not the aim

In terms of his two vital deliveries, the lead has similar concerns to those of the singles player at the start of an end, but not identical. Both are trying to set up a favourable head, but in singles there is considerable pressure to emerge from the first two bowls holding shot. To do so does not always result in winning the end, but with only four bowls to come it is better to be one up (or ideally two up) than one down. It puts pressure on the opponent to change the situation. This is not the case for the lead. With 12 bowls to come there is no great merit in holding shot, at least for its own sake. There will be ample opportunity to convert the head later on, at a time of maximum advantage. What the lead has to do is get two good bowls into the head, positioned in a way that makes life as difficult as possible for the opposition number 2. He must be well up (certainly never short if the opponent is lying shot), not jack-high, of course, and he should guard against taking too tight a line to the jack, since a bowl that swings away in front of the jack is unlikely to contribute further to the proceedings.

If he is holding shot after his first bowl he must be careful not offer a large target by putting his second bowl alongside. Conversely, if his opposite number is holding shot he should try to come right along side, thereby broadening the target for his number 2. Never should he try to remove an opponent's bowl. That is a task for others.

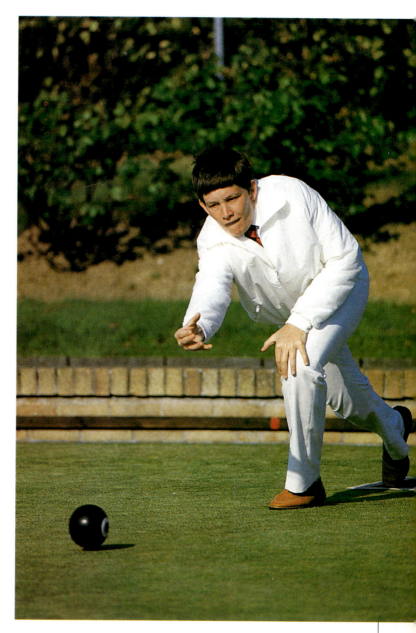

Norfolk's John Ottaway is one of the greatest specialist leads – a position in which he has long represented England on the international stage.

Number 2

It is frequently said that the number 2 is the forgotten man in fours. Sandwiched between the lead, whose function even if underrated is at least plainly understood, and the shakers and movers who follow, the number 2 is easily overlooked.

Astute observers of the game will not fall into this mistake. Having stressed the importance of the lead, that is still the best position for the novice, not just for his sake but because the demands on the number 2 are too great. Apart from his official duty of keeping the scorecard (and checking it at regular intervals with his opposite number), the number 2 is faced with the task of either consolidating a good position or salvaging a bad one.

He comes to the mat to face a situation not of his making. Either his lead has established a solid foundation for the head or he has not. If the former, the number 2 must build on that foundation, hoping to leave his number 3 in a really dominant position. If the latter, he must do everything in his power to retrieve the situation, knowing that if he fails in this task his team-mates may be left chasing a forlorn cause. That is a considerable responsibility.

If the situation is favourable, his skip will either ask him to protect the shot bowl(s) or to get his bowls into the head in such a way as to provide insurance for later developments. Either way, posi-

The number 2 playing red has his final bowl to turn the head to his team's advantage.

SINGLES, PAIRS AND TEAM PLAY

tional shots are called for, so the number 2 must not only be a good draw player but he must also be able to vary line and length at will. This is particularly difficult during the early stages, and the number 2 who is first in the groove will give his team a real boost.

If the head is unfavourable when the number 2 comes to the mat, his course of action is radically different. If the lead has not got a bowl in close, then the skip will direct him to get right into the head, either to take shot or at least to get bowls into position for a conversion later on. Failure to do so can lead to disaster, because it may leave the opposition with a virtually impregnable head.

The number 2 can be described as the anchorman of the side. Unlike the lead, his is anything but a specialist position, calling upon the complete range of shots. Consequently, at the international level the number 2 role is usually taken on by a county skip. It should be noted that it requires an equable temperament to be able to shift easily from giving orders to taking them.

There is a particular practice routine that will give you insight into the the number 2 position, and it is equally useful for singles. Make up a head of four bowls, haphazardly, two aside. Then study it, decide on the percentage shot and play it. Note the result, form another head and so on. This, of course, has more than a little relevance for the singles game.

Unlike the lead, who is left to his own devices for the opening draws, the number 2 awaits instruction from the skip as to what shot he should attempt.

BOWL TO WIN

Number 3

Apart from his bowling and tactical contribution, the number 3 also has the task of marking his skip's touchers, measuring for shots and clearing the rink of 'dead' bowls.

It is impossible to describe the role of the number 3 in purely bowling terms. As far as that aspect is concerned, it is enough to say that the number 3 must be an all-round good bowler, since he will face every conceivable situation when he comes to the mat. In particular he will be called upon to play a wide variety of running shots, so he must be confident of weight. He will be a good singles player, and a number 3 at international level will, like the number 2, probably be a county skip. The number 3 is also tasked with measuring in the head, marking his skip's touchers and removing 'dead' bowls to the bank.

The real key to the position is the number 3's relationship with his skip. It is perhaps best explained with reference to the related winter sport of curling, where the number 3 in the rink is called vice-skip. He is the skip's close partner, his right hand. So the blend of personalities is of crucial importance. All the ingredients that go into any good partnership are wanted, but note that it is not a partnership of equals, on the rink. The number 3 must have confidence in his skip, and vice versa, but he must also be willing to subordinate his decision-making faculty to that of his skip.

The loyal lieutenant

That may not be easy, since the number 3 may be every bit as good a bowler as his skip, and often much better on the day. Nevertheless, he must be the loyal lieutenant come what may. At club level the more senior members tend to gravitate to the lower orders, and human nature being what it is the number 3 may feel he should really be skipping, while the skip may be looking anxiously over his shoulder. If these feel-

SINGLES, PAIRS AND TEAM PLAY

ings prevail, the team will not amount to much. Dissension in a team is ruinous, and even an undercurrent of resentment will damage performance as surely as it will mar the pleasure of the activity.

This is not to say that the number 3 should be a 'yes man'. His job is to advise the skip, and having done so, to accept the skip's decision, whether or not it is in accord with that advice, and support it with complete conviction. His tactical discussions with the skip should take place at the head, and never when the skip is on the mat, when the number 3 should be directing the head. He must also provide the link between the skip and the other team members. There must be easy communication throughout the team, and the lines of communication run through the number 3.

A personal choice

Beyond that it is impossible to say what makes a good number 3. A good number 3 for one skip may be no good for another, for entirely personal reasons. It may be a lack of respect, either way, a clash of personalities or simply a lack of balance between the personalities. For example, if the skip is a reserved, rather quiet type, it would seem desirable for the number 3 to be outgoing. Indeed if there is any generalisation worth making it is that the good number 3 is more likely to be an extrovert than an introvert, because of his role as a communicator. However, if his outgoing personality is too boisterous for the skip's taste, or if he is too free with his advice (from the skip's point of view), what then? In a sense, the best number 3 is the number 3 the skip feels most comfortable and confident playing with. As in all team sports, the personalities must balance.

While the skip determines his own choice of shot, after consultation with his number 3, when he goes to the mat the number 3 assumes command of the head.

Skip

As team leader, the skip has the most important role of the four, indisputably. While his two bowls may not be more important than anyone else's, coming when they do they can hardly be less important. On top of that is placed the burden of directing the team. At the upper reaches of the game this means directing the activities of three players any or all of whom may be his equal in terms of bowling skill, or in some cases possibly his superior.

Good leadership qualities are universal in their application, and they are widely understood – even if not so widely practised. There is no need to dwell on such characteristics as vision, judgment, commitment, firmness, fairness and tact. The good skip will display all these, and any other favourable attributes that circumstances demand.

His primary task is to provide his small band of warriors with purposeful direction. From opening bowl to final shot, his must be the guiding intelligence behind every action. His relationship with each team member will be different, because their functions are different, but in each case his aim must be to enable. He must get the best possible performance from each of his crew, by whatever means. And then he must get the best out of himself as a bowler, leading by example. In every way connected with the enterprise the skip must have the unqualified respect of his teammates, and to enjoy that respect he must deserve it.

The quality of leadership

It is worth looking at the skip in his relationship with each team member in turn, but first consider his relationship with the team as a whole. Team morale is the invaluable byproduct of team confidence. This is not just a matter of confidence in performance, but confidence in the team as an entity. The skip must conduct himself in such a way as to inspire that confidence, which means that he must communicate to the others what it is he wants them to achieve, and make them believe that they can achieve it. He must make them feel totally involved in the corporate activity. Even when they lose, as they must, the morale remains intact.

Therefore, everything that has been said about the necessity for the number 3 to be a good communicator holds true for the skip. It does not matter whether he is of a lively or sober disposition, but he must be effective in getting his views across in a persuasive way. He must give advice where it is helpful, instruc-

The skip indicates exactly where she wants the shot to finish. Such precise instructions are a key element in successful skipping.

tion where it is required and encouragement at all times.

The lead knows what is required of him, so all the skip has to ensure is that the lead goes to the mat in a positive frame of mind. Generally, the skip will select the length of jack he wants the lead to deliver, but not always. At the beginning of the match, for instance, if the skip has no feeling one way or the other he may decide to let the lead choose his own length, since the lead may have hit upon a perfect length during the trial ends. He will not, however, want a short jack to start off with for reasons explained earlier. Thereafter, the skip will want to make the choice because it is a tactical matter involving the team as a whole (bearing in mind the twin objectives of suiting your team and disconcerting the opposition). The same holds true for mat placement. This can be potentially difficult within the team. If, for example, the skip is playing especially well to a particular length then he might opt for that length even if the lead is having difficulty with it. It is imperative that such a tactical decision is seen to be made on objective grounds, not for the greater glory of the skip.

The tactical battle joined

The number 2 now enters the fray. Unless it is too obvious to be worth pointing out, the skip will make the choice of shot, perhaps in consultation with the number 3, and certainly having taken into account his relevant knowledge of the number 2's bowling capacities, hand preference and so on. But it is his choice, since the tactical campaign is on, and the entire tactical responsibility is his. When he gives his instructions, here and everywhere in the course of the match, the skip should do so with clarity and precision, and with confidence. Now and again the skip may have practical advice for the number 2 (or anyone else), which he should not be slow to give, in an appropriate manner. The thoughtful skip will be unfailingly encouraging when a member of the team is struggling.

The skip awaits his number 3's bowl. The skip must call the shot, although he will naturally be loth to ask the number 3 to play against his own judgment.

BOWL TO WIN

The number 3 and the skip are together for most of the match, they should know each other's games inside out, and they should share a joint perception of the situation in which the number 3 must play his bowls. For the most part they will reach a consensus about the shot, but if, following thorough analysis, the skip is convinced that he, and not his number 3, has the truer perception of the situation, then it is right and proper for his view to prevail. Naturally this is a delicate matter, and it would be a foolish skip who made a habit of telling his number 3 to bowl against his own judgement. But it is the skip's prerogative, and when he uses it he has a complete right to expect his number 3 to bow to his judgment and commit himself fully to the shot.

The moment of decision
When the skip comes to bowl himself, the battle moves to its inevitable climax. The tactical considerations can be legion, and the skip will rely on his number 3 to help him clarify his thinking as he weighs the possibilities. Here is where the relationship between the two is at its most critical, and where the number 3 requires a subtle as well as astute mind.

He will want to provide the best possible advice, and he should not shrink from trying to persuade the skip of the correctness of his views. However, not only does the skip have to make the final decision, as always, but this time he has to deliver the bowl himself. The number 3, therefore, has to weigh the objective situation in the head against the subjective nature of the skip's own mind. In other words, even if the number 3 is convinced that he has the better plan, is it so much better than the skip's that it should be pressed beyond a certain point?

This is not so much a matter of tact, since the two of them discuss shot selection endlessly, and it would be a flawed partnership if the skip took such a disagreement personally. It is more a question of enabling the skip to go to the mat certain that he has made the right choice. At this critical juncture that imperative outweighs fine distinctions between choices of shot, and so the number 3 must know when to desist, just as the skip must know when to insist.

The team hovers over the head, willing the skip's bowl home. Such team commitment is the skip's responsibility, just as much as his ability to deliver the vital bowl.

SINGLES, PAIRS AND TEAM PLAY

Triples

This is a curious game, for which some see no need, but which others find uniquely satisfying. It is tactically the same as fours, except that the number 2 has a rather broader canvas to work on than he does in fours, He has frequently been described as a sort of number 2 and 3 rolled into one.

The singular feature of triples is the number of bowls in play. Because each player has three, the head can be cluttered with 18 bowls. That is of course not a huge increase on 16, but it can lead to congestion and a bit of helter-skelter late in the end. There is growing enthusiasm in Australia for two-bowl triples, and this may spread.

KEY POINTS
- *Accurate drawing is the key to singles success*
- *Play to your opponent's weaknesses as well as your own strengths*
- *It is generally wise to avoid heavy shots in the opening stages*
- *If you fall behind, do not resort to 'all or nothing' shots*
- *In pairs, the lead plays every bit as important a role as the skip*
- *A good lead is invariably a good singles player*
- *For the lead, two useful bowls in the head is more important than gaining shot*
- *The number 2 is the anchorman of the team*
- *The number 3 is effectively vice-skip*
- *The skip is solely responsible for tactics*

A triples competition under blue Spanish skies.

THE WINNING FORMULA

Like any competitive activity, the game of bowls cannot be reduced to a series of technical challenges tackled with intelligence infused by experience. It is, of course, all those things, but it is above all a contest, and in any contest psychological strengths and weaknesses are of enormous significance. Of course if there are gross disparities in the level of skills, that is the end of the matter, but in a contest between players of roughly equivalent skills such qualities as composure, determination, coolness under fire and so forth are likely to be decisive.

The psychological battle is won by the player who succeeds in planting the seed of defeat in his opponent's mind, and having done so seizes every opportunity to make that seed grow into a sturdy plant.

At the extremes of human character and personality there are the so-called born winners and born losers. The former seem unshakable in their self belief: they simply exude confidence and in competition they proceed as if the thought of defeat could never cross their minds. They ruthlessly press home every advantage, yet are at their most dangerous in times of crisis, where the threat of danger summons up that indomitable fighting spirit. The latter betray their lack of self-confidence in everything they say or do, as though they are resigned to the familiar state of defeat. Even when victory opens her arms they spurn her, and of course the application of pressure causes a feeble rather than fighting response.

Then there are natural team players. Whatever position they play, their flair for comradeship as well as their unswerving commitment to the enterprise is an invaluable asset, particularly in adversity. Others may be of such a solitary nature as to appear cold and indifferent – casting a shadow wherever they move.

At those extremes any advice given in these pages is either unnecessary or inapplicable. Fortunately, most of us fall into some middle ground, being neither invincible warriors nor defenceless wimps. So it is that there are practical steps you can take to improve your chances of coming out on top in the critical psychological battle.

THE WINNING FORMULA

The Irish international Ian McClure appears almost to be in communion with his bowl, so intense is his concentration.

BOWL TO WIN

MENTAL APPROACH

To begin with, positive thinking at every stage, and in every respect, is vital to success. Play to win, not to avoid defeat. That means setting out to crack your opponent, by all fair means. If the luck seems to be running against you, ignore it, just as you ignore any negative feelings if your opponent forges ahead through superior play. Assume that luck will even out, just as you assume that your skills will inevitably pull you back into the game. Never give any sign that you are rattled or on the run.

Naturally, there will be times when the pressure threatens to get to you, as it does to us all. Even then, there are ways to control it. For example, if you are facing a critical draw shot with your final bowl, that can be a pressure-ridden situation even if you only need to get within two feet of the jack. If it were not for the fact that your opponent holds 3 shots, and they mean game, that draw would be well within your ability, but under the circumstances it is reducing you to a bundle of nerves.

A trick of the mind
Calm down for a moment and try to imagine that those three bowls are indeed yours rather than your opponent's. Even the best of them is not that close to the jack, and if you were drawing to make 4 you would confidently go for the jack and expect to get there. If you can hold that thought in your mind the shot should lose its terror. Now calmly set about drawing to the jack.

Another simple psychological trick, and you can play it all the time, is to expect your opponent to play a perfect shot. If he does, at least you were prepared for it, so it will not come as an unexpected blow. If, as is more likely, his shot is less than perfect, then the situation is bound to be better than you thought it would be, and that should provide you with a boost.

Curbing the imagination
Try not to exercise your imagination in unproductive ways. When your opponent is playing, any number of results may occur. If it is a critical bowl, say his last with yours to follow, it is tempting to speculate about what you are likely to face. Will you be able to squeeze through on the backhand draw, or will

English international Mary Price is a model of positive commitment as she watches her bowl begin its journey.

THE WINNING FORMULA

you find yourself blocked on your favourite hand and have to play a tap and lie on the forehand. Or will the situation require a firing shot, and so on and so on? Do not allow such fevered thoughts to enter your mind. You are only going to have to face one of those scenarios (or maybe one that you had not even considered), so wait for it. The real situation, from moment to moment, is your only sensible concern.

Getting things in focus

You must harness this positive approach with intense concentration. The vogue word in sports circles these days is 'focus' – commentators describe how focused Linford Christie is as he awaits the starter's gun. What they mean is that he has achieved a mental state where nothing is able to intrude on one isolated, insulated task. He looks down the track as though down a tunnel, and every fibre of his being is attuned to exploding from the blocks, and catapulting himself to the finishing line. His concentration is a wonder to behold.

So yours should be as you stand on the mat. You have assessed the situation and made up your mind what you have to do. It cannot be overemphasised that you should never approach the mat until you have done that. And when you get there, if a doubt creeps into your mind, step off the mat and look at the situation again. There is no harm in this, no sign of weakness. It is natural enough to vacillate when facing a tricky shot with various options, but there comes a point at which you have to decide, and you must have arrived at that point before you prepare for the shot. Thereafter, nothing but the execution of that shot, there and then, should be allowed to enter your thoughts. All that has gone before, all that is to come, are irrelevant.

Celebration for the Essex team, having won the Inaugural County Junior Two-Fours Title.

PURPOSEFUL PRACTICE

As does any activity that puts a premium on acquired skills, bowls rewards practice, and this remains true at all levels of the game. In terms of what they actually do themselves, at this stage in their careers, the authors adopt different approaches to practice, but of its undoubted importance they agree fully. And they agree, too, that practice is not a matter of having a casual roll-up, either with a friend or on your own. There is nothing wrong with doing that – good fun and relaxing it can be – but do not confuse it with practice.

Purposeful practice can be defined as practice directed at gaining skill or knowledge of specific aspects of the game, either technical or tactical. Because these two aspects come together when you are playing a game, in assessing the head, selecting the shot and then executing it, only by separating them out on the practice green can you bear down repeatedly on whatever it is that you would like to improve upon, or deepen your understanding of.

Take technique first. If you are a novice, or fairly new to the game, by far

It is indisputable that you will progress further and faster in the game if you establish a good practice routine.

THE WINNING FORMULA

the most important task you face is learning to bowl on line to a length, as has been stressed repeatedly. The only way to develop even modest competence in this requirement is to practice. Take a session and work solely on line, spend another on length, another putting them together, and so on. Every technical aspect of the game that has been explained in these pages not only rewards practice, it positively demands it, however naturally gifted you may be.

Looking for improvement

If you are an experienced bowler, you will inevitably have (relatively) weak points in your technique. You may have a backhand that tends to break down under pressure, or a tendency to hook your forehand. Or a part of your game that has been serving you well suddenly begins causing you problems under match conditions. However you view your technical proficiency, it is difficult to imagine that you are equally content with every aspect of it, and purposeful practice is obviously your shortest route to improvement.

On the tactical side, bowls throws up all manner of situations that puzzle any bowler. Through repeated play you begin to develop a memory bank, and this experience forms the basis for tactical decision-making. Even if you must accept that no two heads are ever identical, you do see similarities between them, and by drawing on your memory bank you have a pretty good idea that a particular shot is likely to give a good result, or another, superficially attractive, has a potential sting in the tail.

Nevertheless, even if you become as experienced as the authors you will still encounter heads where it is not at all clear what the percentage shot is, or where you play a shot as you intended and get a surprising result. The point is that your memory bank is potentially infinite in capacity, and if you want to be a serious player you should consciously try to expand it.

Where practice comes in is that it enables you to progress in this life-long learning process away from the heat of battle. You can try to recreate heads that provoked your curiosity, or create new and interesting ones, and then bowl to them. If you do not like the result, you can put the bowls back and play it differently, again and again until you think you have a thorough understanding of that type of head.

The purpose in mind

Practising alone or with a partner can be equally effective. Solo practice enables you to be more singleminded, because you do not have to make any allowances for your partner's agenda. However, congenial company can pay dividends, because your partner may be able to bring deficiencies of technique to your attention, and provide fresh insights into the analysis of heads.

In either case, make it a firm rule to practice only to the point that you are concentrating completely on your purpose. The moment you feel any aimlessness or boredom creeping into it, head for the clubhouse. Otherwise you are wasting your time. And finally, it is a firm maxim of David Bryant's, whose authority on this as on other matters is universally acknowledged, that you should always complete your practice session on a good end. Quit on a good note, while you can feel that you're ahead and improving.

BRYANT ON PRACTICE

Like Tony, I was born into a bowling family. My grandfather was a founder member of my own Clevedon club, and a county player, and my father was a regular Middleton skip for Somerset and represented England as an Indoor International. With that heritage, it is scarcely surprising that I was fascinated by bowls at a very young age, was an avid spectator and fantasised endlessly about performing great feats in the game. Very early on I acquired a discarded set of bowls, and set to work practising on our very uneven, sloping front garden. From that time to this I have never ceased practising the game I love, and have been fortunate to make my career.

'At the upper echelons of any sport there are marked differences between the extent to which players practise. I am firmly in the Nick Faldo and Bjorn Borg camp, believing that practice makes perfect. In my view (and it is borne out by my own experience), the surest way to get to the top, and stay there, is to develop the mechanical aspect of the game to a pitch of perfect consistency, within human limits. Only then, with the mechanics so ingrained as to require no thought, is the mind free to concentrate solely on the dynamics of the match. I say big matches are won on the practice green by the player who ignores the gathering gloom or the rain when others have retreated to the comfort of the clubhouse.

'I will go further and positively recommend practising under the most adverse possible circumstances. Inclement weather, noise, distractions of all sort, these 'assault course' conditions are the best way to acquire the self-discipline to cope with the intense pressures of match play. Concentration and control under fire are the rewards, and the implied analogy with combat training is perfectly appropriate. Not, I hasten to add, that I see competitive bowls as war, only that it requires qualities of resolution and grit, and while they may be in some measure innate, I believe that with practice it is possible to acquire them.'

David Bryant has been a life-long devotee as well as advocate of purposeful practice.

ALLCOCK ON PRACTICE

'I would happily put my name to everything that is ever said about the value of purposeful practice, and in my youth I practised like a demon. I have explained earlier how I worked so hard to develop my ability to pick line, bowling over the handkerchief. And how I scattered jacks at random, to ingrain an ability to bowl to length. I can't imagine that anyone ever showed more persistence than I did to acquire the skills of my trade.

'However, I must confess that since I reached the top levels of the sport I have practised little. This somewhat eccentric behaviour is not, I believe, the result of laziness, far less is it creeping boredom with the act of bowling. I love bowling, but still I choose not to practice very much. Naturally if there is some aspect of my game that is troubling me I will go to the practice green to try to sort it out. But that is the exception, not the rule, and it does not add up to the consistent practice advocated by any serious coach or student of the game – including me!

'There are, I think, two basic reasons for my attitude, although they are probably connected. First, my technique is in many ways unorthodox, as I have explained in the relevant sections. I persist with my quirks because they work for me, and have never, in my opinion, hampered my play. There are any number of reasons why I lose matches, but not because I flick my wrist, or 'sense' line and so on. If I thought otherwise, then I would be forced to go to the practice green with a vengeance. I would virtually have to dismantle my technique – an appalling prospect! If that were ever to happen then I would have to cope with it, but as long as I feel confident in my 'instinctive' ability to bowl, I shall persist. And what would feel to me the grind of

Tony Allcock is himself something of a stranger to the practice green – but he knows its value well.

daily practice would add little to my confidence in my instinctive ability.

'Secondly, while I dearly love bowling, my appetite for it is not unlimited. I am more afraid of getting stale through bowling too much than I am of getting rusty by bowling too little. And such is the schedule of a professional bowler that I get to bowl enough for my tastes. I do not want to give the impression that I think I know everything there is to know about bowls. No one can. I simply think that for me, and I stress the personal nature of these comments, more, in the context of regular practice, would mean less. But if you want to take the best advice, as usual I recommend that you take David's!'

SPORTSMANSHIP

Bowlers are fortunate to participate in a sport that has throughout its history been conducted by a high code of behaviour. It is not only a game played to a set of rules, but it has a very definite etiquette. It is similar to golf in this respect, and similar too in that it breeds good friendships, both on and off the field of play.

It is a good idea to take the trouble to study the laws of the game, so as not to make unintentional gaffes during the (short) period of initiation. There are, however, a few simple things that even more experienced players might take note of in terms of maximising enjoyment for all on the rink. For example, it is sporting to give your opponents an unimpeded view of the line your bowl takes along the green, and if you are running alongside the bowl it is quite easy to position yourself so as not to obscure that view. It is important to give your opponents immediate possession of the rink once your bowl has come to rest (allowing time to chalk a toucher), and it is equally important never to stand in a position that might distract an opposing

Good sportsmanship means acknowledging your opponent's good shots with warm applause, not sullen acceptance.

THE WINNING FORMULA

bowler. Obviously, it is a gross breach of etiquette (not to mention the rules) to do anything to put a bowler off.

This can happen by accident, and it can then raise a potential problem. For instance, in singles play, one player may be of an extrovert nature, friendly, chatty and so forth – not in any way an exponent of gamesmanship, just that sort of outgoing personality. If the opponent is of similar temperament, or at any rate finds this kind of behaviour quite acceptable, well and good. But if the opponent prefers to play a match with minimal (though courteous) contact, he really should be allowed to do so. To persist with unwanted chitchat in such circumstances is poor sportsmanship, and if you do so you invite a firm request by your opponent that you respect his right to play the game in what you might well consider an unsociable spirit.

These are just a few arbitrary examples of the code of good manners and good sportsmanship that must always infuse the game. The golden rule, of course, is to behave towards others as you would want them to behave towards you. This is just as true after a match as it is during. If there is anything worse than a bad loser it is a bad winner. The one sulks, which is ill-mannered but just about bearable. The other gloats, which is quite unforgivable. Modesty in victory, generosity in defeat, that is the rule.

KEY POINTS
- *Always play positively to win*
- *Do not waste mental energy speculating about future developments*
- *Be fully committed to the shot before going to the mat*
- *Practise for a specific purpose*
- *Stop practice on a good end*
- *Be a good winner as well as a good loser – you are bound to have plenty of experience of both*

Andy Thomson acknowledges the cheers as he reaches the pinnacle of the bowling world – World Indoors Singles Champion for 1994.

GLOSSARY

Across the head
A shot that arrives narrow of the head, if intentional usually with the aim of taking an opposition bowl out of the COUNT, if unintentional likely to be a wasted bowl.

Aiming point
The visual mark towards which a bowler directs his delivery in order to achieve the desired result. It may be a real object (something on the bank) or it may be the imaginary SHOULDER OF THE ARC, or it may be any point on the rink along the perceived line the bowl should take (eg a patch of discoloured grass). Whatever it is, it is what the bowler delivers to, not the position he desires the bowl to reach.

Arc
The curve the bowl describes as it responds to the BIAS.

Athletic stance
A generally upright stance from which the delivery is made. The feet should be in line with the intended delivery, and the delivery is made by bending the knees and stepping forward to ground the bowl, with the follow through as a natural extension of the movement. This is the most natural of stances for the able-bodied bowler, and in some form, as modified to suit individual requirements, it is by far the most common stance.

Attacking bowl
As the term implies, a bowl played with hostile intent, often a DRIVE, either directed at an individual opposition bowl or into the HEAD in such a way as to alter it to the bowler's advantage.

Back bowl
A bowl well behind the jack, intentionally played as a safeguard against the eventuality of the jack being displaced. The 'best' back bowl is the one nearest the ditch, a good thing to have if the jack is ditched.

Banks
The raised perimeter of the green beyond the ditch, and therefore out of bounds.

Bias
The lateral force acting on the bowl in the course of its journey which gives it the characteristic arc. The term is often used to describe the running characteristics of the bowl itself, and is a feature of bowls manufacture – the off-centre centre of gravity. There is a minimum bias established by a MASTER BOWL, against which all bowls must be tested, but no maximum. Natural bias is affected by playing conditions (green type, wind, etc).

Block shot
A bowl deliberately positioned short of the head and, in normal circumstances, as close as possible to the centre line, in order to deprive the opponent of direct access to the head. The 'blocker' is one of the most destructive of POSITIONAL SHOTS.

Claw grip
The most popular means of holding the bowl in the course of the delivery. The thumb is positioned high up the side of the bowl (on or near the grip, if the bowl has one). The bowl rests forward of the palm, most of its weight on the fingers.

Count
The number of shots scored on an end – usually employed to describe a high tally.

Cradle grip
The alternative to the claw, in which the bowl is 'cradled' in the palm of the hand

GLOSSARY

with the thumb dropped. Sometimes modified by bringing the thumb partly up the side. It is often the choice of bowlers brought up in heavy green conditions because it affords maximum power with minimum effort. On a FAST GREEN the fact that it gives less control puts it at a disadvantage.

Crouch stance
The stance immortalised by David Bryant (with or without curved pipe), in which the bowler crouches on the mat before rising to deliver the bowl. Because the bowler rises to a greater or lesser extent, depending on the power that must be put behind the shot, it is in fact a preamble to the athletic stance. The reason for putting the knees through a lifetime of strain is that its proponents find it helps them pick out the line for delivery – rather as golfers crouch to line up putts.

Dead bowl
A bowl that finishes outside the boundaries of play (in the ditch or outside the strings), and is immediately removed to the bank. The exception is of course the TOUCHER in the ditch.

Dead end
An end is declared dead if the jack is driven beyond the boundaries of play (unless it is in the ditch, between the strings). The end is replayed, in the same direction.

Ditching the jack
Driving the jack into the ditch, which does or does not result in a dead end, depending upon whether the jack remains within the side perimeters of the rink.

Draw shot
The basic and most important shot in the game, in which the bowl is delivered as close as possible to the jack. Frequently a bowler will draw to some other part of the rink, in which case the shot is better described as a positional shot.

Drive shot
Also known as a firing shot, it is played with great force in order to remove one or more bowls from the head, or simply to shake up an adverse head. It is delivered hard enough to negate bias, so is aimed directly at the target. The drive is generally employed late in an end, often as a desperate remedy. An accurate drive is a devastating weapon, but should be used sparingly.

Fast green
A surface that presents little resistance to the bowl, which means that little effort is needed to get the bowl to the other end. The fastest greens are in the Southern Hemisphere, especially in New Zealand.

Firm wood
A bowl played with considerable force, but not a full-blooded drive. Unlike the drive, the firm wood is affected by bias, so is not delivered straight to the target.

Finger grip
An extreme version of the claw grip, in which the bowl is held completely clear of the palm, well forward in the fingers, which take all the weight. The thumb comes right to the top of the bowl. This grip combines maximum sensitivity with minimum power, and is much favoured on those lightning-fast New Zealand greens.

Fixed stance
The body position adopted by a bowler who chooses to restrict the entire delivery action to arm and shoulder. The front foot has completed its full step prior to the delivery, and the free hand steadies the body by gripping the knee or thigh. Able-bodied bowlers do not favour it, because the stability is

England's John Bell holds the bowl in a claw grip.

145

BOWL TO WIN

achieved by sacrificing a great deal of power. For the physically handicapped, of course, it may be the only option, and many employ it to great effect.

Full-length jack
A jack delivered to within two yards of the ditch. It is then centred on the two-yard mark.

Grassing the bowl
The act of (smoothly) placing the bowl on the surface during the delivery.

Green speed
The time, measured in seconds, that it takes a bowl to travel 30 yards to the jack and stop there. The faster the green, the longer it takes to make that journey and pull up, so the higher the green speed. The norm for the British Isles is 10-12 seconds. It can reach double that in the Southern Hemisphere, and in New Zealand green speeds approaching 30 seconds have been recorded. Indoor carpets are generally around the 15-second mark.

Head
The collection of bowls around the jack as the end progresses. In theory, the head comprises all bowls delivered to date, although in practice the term is used to describe only the bowls near enough the jack to be likely to figure in future developments.

Heavy green
A surface that presents considerable resistance to the bowl, and is therefore slow. A normally fast green will be heavy under wet conditions (or if ill-prepared), but generally speaking the heaviest greens are found in Scotland.

Jack high bowl
A bowl level with the jack, to either side.

Lignum vitae
The extremely dense wood from which bowls used to be made. Composition bowls are now the norm.

Live bowl
Any bowl within the confines of the rink or a toucher in the ditch between the strings.

Master Bowl
The international testing bowl which describes the minimum permitted arc under bench-test conditions. All bowls used in competition must be tested against it.

Positional shot
A draw shot played not to the jack but to a predetermined position on the rink (eg a block shot). It is a tactical shot, the intention being to develop the head in such a way as to gain maximum advantage at the completion of the end.

Rest shot
A draw shot to a bowl in the head, usually the shot bowl, the intention being to 'rest' against it in such a position as to gain shot.

Running
A term used to describe the desired WEIGHT of shot (above draw weight). 'Play it with a couple of yards of running', for example.

Running shots
All shots played with greater than draw weight – from the gentlest TAP AND LIE to the most venomous drive.

The head is the collection of bowls in the vicinity of the jack.

GLOSSARY

Semi-crouch stance
Perhaps better described as the low athletic stance, it is basically upright, except that the bowler bends his knees, or back, or both, prior to the delivery.

Shot bowl
The bowl in the head that is, at any juncture, closest to the jack.

Shoulder of the arc
The point at the extreme width of the arc, at which the bowl turns inwards towards the head. The true shoulder is the point at which this actually happens. The imaginary shoulder is the point at which the bowler must aim in order to reach the true shoulder, and it always lies outside the true shoulder.

Springing the jack
The act of knocking the jack away from a bowl it is touching by striking that bowl.

South African Clinic
Also called the semi-fixed stance, it is a variation of the fixed stance. The front foot has partially completed its step, but the weight is kept on the back foot prior to delivery. The step is completed during the delivery, as in the athletic. It is very popular in south Africa, where it was developed by the noted bowls theoretician Dr Julius Serge.

Straight hand
Never literally the case, but often either the forehand or backhand tends to be running straighter than its opposite, and is called the straight hand.

Tap and lie shot
A shot played with slightly more than draw weight, with the objective of 'tapping' a bowl out of the way and 'lying' in its place. Its alternative name is the wrest shot, 'wresting' position from the object bowl.

Tied end
If the measure for shot cannot separate two bowls the end is declared tied, and not replayed.

Toucher
A bowl which in its original course on the green touches the jack. It is marked with chalk to denote its status as a 'toucher', and it remains live even if it subsequently ends up in the ditch (between the strings). A toucher can be very valuable in the event of a ditched jack.

Tracking
A flattening of the playing surface along the principal lines of play. The area tracking runs faster, significantly so after prolonged play, especially in wet conditions. To a much lesser extent, tracking can occur on indoor rinks.

Trail shot
A running shot which strikes the jack and takes it through the head – difficult to achieve, but a wonderful stroke if you hold good back bowls.

Weight
The momentum imparted to the bowl during the delivery.

Wick shot
Like the cannon in snooker, a deflection off another bowl. Whether played deliberately, or accepted as a fluke, it can magically transform the position.

World Bowls Board
The governing body of the outdoor game. National associations sometimes modify WBB regulations to suit local conditions, but all international competitions take place in accordance with the WBB Laws.

Yard on shot
A shot played with a yard more than draw weight (ie a little stronger than a tap and lie). The term is often used imprecisely, to mean 'just a little running'.

LAWS OF THE GAME

An understanding of the Laws of the game is essential to its enjoyment. The situation with Bowls is complicated by the fact that the various national associations are entitled to modify the codes of laws set down by the World Bowls Board (WBB) in accordance with domestic conditions. What this means is that if you Bowl in anything other than international competitions governed by the WBB, you will play according to national rules (outdoor or indoor). The World Indoor Bowls Council too stipulates its own rules. Nevertheless, all sets of rules are derived from the WBB Laws, which can be taken as the basis of the game wherever it is played. We thank the WBB for kindly allowing us to reproduce the Laws of the Game.

DEFINITIONS

1. (a) 'Controlling Body' means the body having immediate control of the conditions under which a match is played. The order shall be:
   (i) The World Bowls Board.
   (ii) The National Bowling Authority.
   (iii) Divisions within National Authorities.
   (iv) The club on whose Green the Match is played.
(b) 'Skip' means the player who, for the time being, is in charge of the head on behalf of the team.
(c) 'Team' means either a Four, Triples or a Pair.
(d) 'Side' means any agreed number of teams, whose combined scores determine the results of the match.
(e) 'Four' means a team of four players whose positions in order of playing are named Lead, Second, Third, Skip.
(f) 'Bowl in Course' means a Bowl from the time of its delivery until it comes to rest.
(g) 'End' means the playing of the Jack and all the Bowls of all the opponents in the same direction on a rink.
(h) 'Head' means the Jack and such Bowls as have come to rest within the boundary of the rink and are not dead.
(i) 'Mat Line' means the edge of the Mat which is nearest to the front ditch. From the centre of the Mat Line all necessary measurements to Jack or Bowls shall be taken.
(j) 'Master Bowl' means a Bowl which has been approved by the WBB as having the minimum bias required, as well as in all other respects complying with the Laws of the Game and is engraved with the words Master Bowl.
   (i) A standard Bowl of the same bias as the Master Bowl shall be kept in the custody of each National Authority.
   (ii) A standard Test Bowl shall be provided for the use of each official Licensed Tester.
(k) 'Jack High' means that the nearest portion of the Bowl referred to is in line with and at the same distance from the Mat Line as the nearest portion of the Jack.
(l) 'Pace of Green' means the number of seconds taken by a Bowl from the time of its delivery to the moment it comes to rest, approximately 90 feet (27.43 metres) from the Mat Line.
(m) 'Displaced' as applied to a Jack or Bowl means 'disturbed' by any agency that is not sanctioned by these laws.
(n) 'A set of Bowls' means four Bowls all of a material set which are of the same manufacture and are of the same, size, weight, colour, bias and where applicable serial number and engraving.

THE GREEN

2. The Green – Area and Surface
The Green should form a square of not less than 120 feet (36.58 metres) and not more than 132 feet (40.23 metres) a side. It shall have a suitable natural playing surface which shall be level. It shall be provided with suitable boundaries in the form of a ditch and bank.

3. The Ditch
The Green shall be surrounded by a ditch which shall have a holding surface not injurious to Bowls and be free from obstacles. The ditch shall be not less than 8 inches (203mm) nor more than 15 inches (381mm) wide and it shall be not less than 2 inches (51mm) nor more than 8 inches (203mm) below the level of the green.

4. Banks
The bank shall be not less than 9 inches (229mm) above the level of the green, preferably upright, or alternatively at an angle of not more than 35 degrees from the perpendicular. The surface of the face of the bank shall be non-injurious to Bowls. No steps likely to interfere with play shall be cut in the banks.

5. Division of the Green
The Green shall be divided into spaces called rinks, each not more than 19 feet (5.79 metres), nor less than 18 feet (5.48 metres), wide. They shall be numbered consecutively, the centre line of each rink being marked on the bank at each end by a wooded peg or other suitable device. The four corners of the rinks shall be marked by pegs made of wood, or other suitable material, painted white and fixed to the face of the bank and flush therewith or alternatively fixed on the bank not more than 4 inches (102mm) back from the face thereof. The corner pegs shall be connected by a green thread drawn tightly along one surface of the green, with sufficient loose thread to reach the

LAWS OF THE GAME

corresponding pegs on the face or surface of the bank, in order to define the boundary of the rink.

White pegs or discs shall be fixed on the side banks to indicate a clear distance of 76 feet (23.16 metres) from the ditch on the line of play. Under no circumstances shall the boundary thread be lifted while the Bowl is in motion. The boundary pegs of an outside rink shall be placed at least 2 feet (61cm) from the side ditch.

6. Permissible Variations of Laws 2 and 5
(a) National Authorities may admit greens not longer than 44 yards (40.23 metres), nor shorter than 33 yards (30.17 metres) in the direction of play.
(b) For domestic play the Green may be divided into Rinks, not less than 14 feet (4.27 metres) nor more than 19 feet (5.79 metres) wide. National Associations may dispense with the use of boundary threads.
(c) National Authorities may approve artificial surfaces for domestic play.

MAT, JACK, BOWLS, FOOTWEAR

7. Mat
The mat shall be of a definite size, namely 24 inches (61cm) long and 14 inches (35.6cm) wide.

8. Jack
The Jack shall be round and white or yellow in colour, with a diameter of not less than 2 15/32nd inches (63mm), nor more than 2 17/32nd inches (64mm) and not less than 8oz (227 gr), nor more than 10oz (283 gr) in weight.

9. Bowls
(a) (i) Bowls shall be made of wood, rubber or composition and shall be black or brown in colour, and each Bowl of the set shall bear the member's individual and distinguishing mark on each side. The provision relating to the distinguishing mark on each side of the Bowl need not apply other than in International Matches, World Bowls Championships and Commonwealth Games. Bowls made of wood (lignum vitae) shall have a maximum diameter of 5 1/4 inches (134mm) and a minimum diameter of 4 9/16 inches (116mm) and the weight shall not exceed 3lb 8oz (1.59kg). Loading of Bowls made of wood is strictly prohibited.
(ii) For all International and Commonwealth Games Matches, a Bowl made of rubber or composition shall have a maximum diameter of 5 1/8 inches (130mm) and a minimum diameter of 4 9/16 inches (116mm) and the weight shall not exceed 3lb 8oz (1.59kg).
Subject to Bowls bearing a current stamp of the Board and/or a current stamp of a Member National Authority and/or the current stamp of the BIBC and provided they comply with the Board's Laws, they may be used in all matches controlled by the Board or by any Member National Authority.

Notwithstanding the aforegoing provisions, any member National Authority may adopt a different scale of weights and sizes of Bowls to be used in matches under its own control – such Bowls may not be validly used in International Matches, World Bowls Championships, Commonwealth Games or other matches controlled by the Board if they differ from the Board's Laws and unless stamped with a current stamp of the Board or any Member National Authority or the

Rule 7 states that The mat shall be of a definite size, namely 24 inches (61cm) long and 14 inches (35.6cm) wide.

BIBC.

(iii) The controlling body may, at its discretion, supply and require players to temporarily affix an adhesive marking to their Bowls in any competition game. Any temporary marking under this Law shall be regarded as part of the Bowl for all purposes under these Laws.

(b) Bias of Bowls

The Master Bowl shall have a bias approved by the World Bowls Board. A Bowl shall have a bias not less than that of the Master Bowl, and shall bear the imprint of the stamp of the International Bowling Board/World Bowls Board, or that of its National Authority. National Authorities may adopt a standard which exceeds the bias of the Master Bowl. To ensure accuracy of bias and visibility of stamp, all Bowls shall be re-tested and re-stamped at least once every ten years, or earlier if the date of the stamp is not clearly legible.

(c) Bowls Failing Test

If a Bowl in the hands of a Licensed Tester has been declared as not complying with Law 9(b), it shall be altered, if possible, so as to comply, before being returned. The owner of the Bowls shall be responsible for the expense involved.

If the Bowl cannot be altered to comply with Law 9(a) and (b) any current official stamp appearing thereon shall be cancelled prior to its return. The stamp shall be cancelled by the Tester by stamping an X over any current official stamp. Bowls submitted for testing must be in sets of four.

(d) Objection to Bowls

A challenge may be lodged by an opposing player and/or by the Official Umpire and/or the Controlling Body.

A challenge or any intimation thereof shall not be lodged with any opposing player during the progress of the Match.

A challenge may be lodged with Umpire at any time during a Match, provided the Umpire is not a Player in that or any other match of the same competition.

If a challenge be lodged it shall be made not later than 10 minutes after the completion of the final end in which the Bowl was used.

Once a challenge is lodged with the Umpire, it cannot be withdrawn.

The challenge shall be based on the grounds that the Bowl does not comply with one or more of the requirements set out in Law 9(a) and (b).

The Umpire shall request the user of the Bowl to surrender it to him for forwarding to the Controlling Body. If the owner of the challenged Bowl refuses to surrender it to the Umpire, the Match shall thereupon be forfeited to the opponent. The user or owner, or both, may be disqualified from playing in any match controlled or permitted by the Controlling body, so long as the Bowl remains untested by a Licensed Tester.

On receipt of the Bowls, the Umpire shall take immediate steps to hand them to the Secretary of the Controlling Body, who shall arrange for a table test to be made as soon as practicable, and in the presence of a representative of the Controlling Body.

If a table test be not readily available, and any delay would unduly interfere with the progress of the competition, then, should an approved green testing device be available, it may be used to make an immediate test on the green. If a green test be made it shall be done by, or in the presence of the Umpire over a distance of not less than 70 feet (21.35 metres). The comparison shall be between the challenged Bowl and the standard WBB Test Bowl, or if it be not readily available then a Bowl bearing a current stamp, of similar size or nearly so, should be used.

The decision of the Umpire, as a result of the test, shall be final and binding for that match.

The result of the subsequent table test shall not invalidate the decision given by the Umpire on the green test.

If a challenged Bowl, after an official table test, be found to comply with all the requirements of Law 9(a) and (b), it shall be returned to the user or owner.

If the challenged Bowl be found not to comply with Law 9(a) and (b), the match in which it was played shall be forfeited to the opponent.

If a Bowl in the hands of a Licensed Tester has been declared as not complying with Law 9(b), it shall be altered, if possible, so as to comply, before being returned. The owner of the Bowl shall be responsible for the expense involved.

If the Bowl cannot be altered to comply with Law 9(a) and (b), any current official stamp appearing thereon shall be cancelled prior to its return. The stamp shall be cancelled by the Tester by stamping an X over any current official stamp.

(e) Alteration to Bias

A player shall not alter, or cause to be altered, other than by an Official Bowl Tester, the bias of any Bowl, bearing the imprint of the official stamp of the Board, under penalty of suspension from playing for a period to be determined by the Council of the National Authority, of which his club is a member. Such suspension shall be subject to confirmation by the Board, or a Committee thereof appointed for that purpose, and shall be operative among all Authorities in membership with the Board.

10. Footwear

Players, Umpires and Markers shall wear white, brown or black smooth-soled heel-less footwear while playing on the green or acting as Umpires or Markers.

ARRANGING A GAME

11. General form and duration

A game of Bowls shall be played on one rink or on several rinks. It shall consist of a specified number of shots or ends, or shall be played for any period of time as previously arranged.

The ends of the game shall be played alternately in opposite directions excepting as provided in Laws 38, 42, 44, 46 and 47.

LAWS OF THE GAME

12. Selecting the rinks for play
When a match is to be played, the draw for the rinks to be played on shall be made by the Skips or their representatives. In a match for a trophy or where competing Skips have previously been drawn, the draw to decide the numbers of the rinks to be played on shall be made by the visiting Skips or their representatives.

No player in a competition or match shall play on the same rink on the day of such competition or match before play commences under penalty of disqualification.

This Law shall not apply in the case of open Tournaments.

13. Play arrangements
Games shall be organised in the following play arrangements:
(a) As a single game
(b) As a team game.
(c) As a side game.
(d) As a serious single games, team games, or side games.
(c) As a special tournament of games.

14. A single game shall be played on one rink of a Green as a single-handed game by two contending players, each playing two, three or four Bowls singly and alternately.

15. (a) A Pairs game by two contending teams of two players called Lead and Skip according to the order in which they play, and who at each end shall play four Bowls alternately, the Leads first, then the Skips similarly.

(For other than International and Commonwealth Games, players in a Pairs game may play two, three or four Bowls each, as previously arranged by the Controlling Body.)
(b) A Pairs game by two contending teams of two players called Lead and Skip according to the order in which they play, and who at each end shall play four Bowls and may play alternately in the following order: Lead 2 Bowls, Skip 2 Bowls, then repeat this order of play.

16. A Triples game by two contending teams of three players, who shall play two or three Bowls singly and in turn, the Leads playing first.

17. A Fours game by two contending teams of four players, each member playing two Bowls singly and in turn.

18. A side game shall be played by two contending sides, each composed of an equal number of teams/players.

19. Games in series shall be arranged to be played on several and consecutive occasions as:
(a) A series or sequence of games organised in the form of an eliminating competition, and arranged as Singles, Pairs, Triples or Fours.
(b) A series or sequence of side matches organised in the form of a league competition, or an eliminating competition or of Inter-Association matches.

20. A special Tournament of Games

Single games and team games may also be arranged in group form as a special tournament of games in which the contestants play each other in turn, or they may play as paired-off teams of players on one or several greens in accordance with a common time-table, success being adjudged by the number of games won, or by the highest net score in shots in accordance with the regulations governing the Tournament.

21. For International Matches, World Bowls Championships and Commonwealth Games in matches where played.
(i) Singles shall be 25 shots up (shots in excess of 25 shall not count), four Bowls each player, played alternately;
(ii) Pairs shall be 21 ends, four Bowls each player played alternately;
(iii) Triples shall be 18 ends, three Bowls each player, played alternately;
(iv) Fours shall be 21 ends, two Bowls each player, played alternately;
PROVIDED that Pairs, Triples and Fours may be of a lesser number of ends, but in the case of Pairs and Fours there shall not be less than 18 ends and in the case of Triples not less than 15 ends, subject in all cases to the express approval of the Board as represented by its most senior officer present. If there be no officer of the Board present at the time, the decision shall rest with the 'Controlling Body' as defined in Law 1. Any decision to curtail the number of ends to be played shall be made before the commencement of any game, and such decision shall only be made on the grounds of climatic conditions, inclement weather or shortage of time to complete a programme.

22. Awards
Cancelled.

Starting the Game
23. (a) Trial ends
Before start of play in any competition, match or game, or in the resumption of an unfinished competition, match or game on another day, not more than one trial end each way shall be played.
(b) Tossing for opening play
The Captains in a side game or Skips in a team game shall toss to decide which side or team shall play first, but in all singles games the opponents shall toss, the winner of the toss to have the option of decision. In the event of a tied (no score) or a dead end, the first to play in the tied end or dead end shall again play first.

In all ends subsequent to the first the winner of the preceding scoring end shall play first.

24. Placing the Mat
At the beginning of the first end the player to play first shall place the centre line of the mat lengthwise on the centre line of the rink, the front edge of the mat to be 6 feet (1.84 metres) from the ditch. (Where groundsheets are in use

BOWL TO WIN

they shall be placed with the back edge 6 feet (1.84 metres) from the ditch. The mat at the first and every subsequent end shall be placed at the back edge of the sheet – the mat's front edge being 6 feet (1.84 metres) from the ditch.).

25. The Mat and its replacement
After play has commenced in any end the mat shall not be moved from its first position.

If the mat be displaced during the progress of an end it shall be replaced as near as practicable in the same position.

If the mat be out of alignment with the centre line of the rink it may be straightened at any time during the end. After the last Bowl in each end has come to rest in play, or has sooner became dead, the mat shall be lifted and placed wholly beyond the face of the rear bank. Should the mat be picked up by a player before the end has been completed, the opposing player shall have the right of replacing the mat in its original position.

26. The Mat and Jack in subsequent ends.
(a) In all subsequent ends the front edge of the mat shall be not less than 6 feet (1.84 metres) from the rear ditch and the front edge of the mat not less than 76 feet (23.16 metres) from the front ditch and on the centre line of the rink of play.
(b) Should the Jack be improperly delivered under Law 30, the opposing player may then move the mat in the line of play, subject to Clause (a) above and deliver the Jack, but shall not play first. Should the Jack be improperly delivered twice by each player in any end, it shall not be delivered again in that end, but shall be centred so that the front of the Jack is a distance of 6 feet (1.84 metres) from the opposite ditch, and the mat placed at the option of the first to play.

If after the Jack is set at regulation length from the ditch (6 feet or 1.84 metres), both players each having improperly delivered the Jack twice, the end is made dead, the winner of the preceding scoring end shall deliver the Jack when the end is played anew.
(c) No one shall be permitted to challenge the legality of the original position of the mat after the first to play has delivered the first Bowl.

27. Stance on Mat
A player shall take his stance on the mat, and at the moment of delivering the Jack or his Bowl, shall have one foot remaining entirely within the confines of the mat. The foot may be either in contact with, or over, the mat. Failure to observe this Law constitutes foot faulting.

28 Foot-faulting
Should a player infringe the Law of foot-faulting the Umpire may, after having given a warning, have the Bowl stopped and declared dead. If the Bowl has disturbed the head, the opponent shall have the option of either resetting the head, leaving the head as altered or declaring the end dead.

29 Delivering the Jack
The player to play first shall deliver the Jack. If the Jack in its original course comes to rest at a distance of less than six feet (1.84 metres) from the opposite ditch, it shall be moved out to a mark at that distance so that the front of the jack is 6 feet (1.84 metres) from the front

You should use the mat to suit your own game – and if that means you are more comfortable bowling from its back end, then do so.

LAWS OF THE GAME

ditch, with the nearest portion of the Jack to the mat line being 6 feet (1.84 metres) from the edge of the opposite ditch.

If the Jack during its original course be obstructed or deflected by a neutral object or person, or by a Marker, Opponent, or member of the opposing team, it shall be re-delivered by the same player. If it be obstructed or deflected by a member of his own tea, it shall be redelivered by the Lead of the opposing team, who shall be entitled to reset the mat.

30. Jack improperly delivered
Should the Jack in any end be not delivered from a proper stance on the mat, or if it ends its original course in the ditch or outside the side boundary of the rink, or less than 70 feet (21.35 metres) in a straight line of play from the edge of the mat, it shall be returned and the opposing player shall deliver the Jack, but shall not play first.

The Jack shall be returned if it is improperly delivered, but the right of the player first delivering the Jack in that end, to play the first Bowl of the end shall not be affected.

No one shall be permitted to challenge the legality of the original length of the Jack after the first to play has delivered the first Bowl.

31. Variation to Laws 24, 26, 29 and 30
Notwithstanding anything contained in Laws 24, 26, 29 and 30, any National Authority may for domestic purposes, but not in any International Matches, World Bowls Championships or Commonwealth games, vary any of the distances mentioned in these Laws.

MOVEMENT OF BOWLS

32. 'Live Bowl'
A Bowl which, in its original course on the green, comes to rest within the boundaries of the rink, and not less than 45 feet (13.71 metres) from the front edge of the mat, shall be accounted as a 'Live' Bowl and shall be in play.

33. 'Touchers'
A Bowl which, in its original course on the green, touches the Jack, even though such Bowl passes into the ditch within the boundaries of the rink, shall be counted as a 'live' Bowl and shall be called a 'toucher'. If after having come to rest a Bowl falls over and touches the Jack before the next succeeding Bowl is delivered, or if in the case of the last Bowl of an end it falls and touches the Jack within the period of 30 seconds invoked under Law 53, such Bowl shall also be a 'toucher'. No Bowl shall be accounted a 'toucher' by playing on to, or by coming into contact with, the Jack while the Jack is in the ditch. If a 'toucher' in the ditch cannot be seen from the mat its position may be marked by a white or coloured peg about 2 inches (51mm) broad placed upright on the top of the bank and immediately in line with the place where the 'toucher' rests.

34. Marking a 'Toucher'
A 'toucher' shall be clearly marked with a chalk mark by a member of the player's team. If, in the opinion of either Skip, or opponent in Singles, a 'toucher' or a wrongly chalked Bowl comes to rest in such a position that the act

Delivering a jack at a length that suits your play, or the play of your team, is an important part of winning at bowls.

of making a chalk mark, or of erasing it, is likely to move the Bowl or to alter the head, the Bowl shall not be marked or have its mark erased but shall be indicated as a 'toucher' or 'non-toucher' as the case may be. If a Bowl is not so marked or not so indicated before the succeeding Bowl comes to rest it ceases to be a 'toucher'. If both Skips or Opponents agree that any subsequent movement of the Bowl eliminates the necessity for continuation of the indicated provision the Bowl shall thereupon be marked or have the chalk erased as the case may be. Care should be taken to remove the 'toucher' marks from all Bowls before they are played, but should a player fail to do so, and should the Bowl not become a 'toucher' in the end in play, the marks shall be removed by the opposing Skip or his deputy or marker immediately the Bowl comes to rest unless the Bowl is indicated as a 'non-toucher' in circumstances governed by earlier provisions of this Law.

35. Movements of 'Touchers'
A 'toucher' in play in the ditch may be moved by the impact of a Jack in play or of another 'toucher' in play, and also by the impact of a 'non-toucher' which remains in play after the impact, and any movement of the 'toucher' by such incidents shall be valid. However should the 'non-toucher' enter the ditch at any time after the impact, it shall be dead, and the 'toucher' shall be deemed to have been displaced by a dead Bowl and provisions of Law 38(e) shall apply.

36. Bowl Accounted 'Dead'
(a) Without limiting the application of any other of these Laws, a Bowl shall be accounted dead if:
   (i) not being a 'toucher', it comes to rest in ditch or rebounds on to the playing surface of the rink after contact with the bank or with the Jack or a 'toucher' in the ditch, or
   (ii) after completing its original course, or after being moved as a result of play, it comes to rest wholly outside the boundaries of the playing surface of the rink, or within 45 feet (13.71 metres) of the front of the mat, or
   (iii) in its original course, pass beyond a side boundary of the rink on a bias which would prevent its re-entering the rink. (A Bowl is not rendered 'dead' by a player carrying it whilst inspecting the head.)
(b) Skips or Opponents in Singles shall agree on the question as to whether or not a Bowl is 'dead'. Any member of either team may request a decision from the Skips, but no member shall remove any Bowl prior to agreement by the Skips. Once their attention has been drawn to the matter, the Skips by agreement must make a decision. If they cannot reach agreement, the Umpire must make an immediate decision.

37. Bowl Rebounding
Only 'Touchers' rebounding from the face of the bank to the ditch or to the rink shall remain in play.

38. Bowl displacement
(a) Displacement by rebounding 'non-toucher' – Bowl displaced by a 'non-toucher' rebounding from the bank shall be restored as near as possible to its original position by a member of the opposing team or by the Marker.
(b) Displacement by participating player – if a Bowl, while in motion or at rest on the green, or a 'toucher' in the ditch, be interfered with or displaced by one of the players, the opposing Skip shall have the option of:
   (i) restoring the Bowl as near as possible to its original position;
   (ii) letting it remain where it rests;
   (iii) declaring the Bowl 'dead';
   (iv) or declaring the end dead;
(c) Displacement by a neutral object or neutral person (other than as provided in clause (d) hereof):
   (i) of a Bowl in its original course – if such a Bowl be displaced within the boundaries of the rink of play without having disturbed the head, it shall be replayed. If it be displaced and it has disturbed the head, the Skips, or the Opponents in Singles, shall reach agreement on the final position of the displaced Bowl and on the replacement of the head, otherwise the end shall be dead.
   These provisions shall also apply to a Bowl in its original course displaced outside the boundaries of the rink of play provided such Bowl was running on a bias which would have enabled it to re-enter the rink.
   (ii) of a Bowl at rest, or in motion as a result of play after being at rest – if such a Bowl be displaced, the Skips, or Opponents in Singles, shall come to an agreement as to the position of the Bowl and of the replacement of any part of the head disturbed by the displaced Bowl, otherwise the end shall be dead.
(d) Displacement inadvertently produced – if a Bowl be moved at the time of its being marked or measured it shall be restored to its former position by opponent. If such displacement is caused by a Marker or an Umpire, the Marker or Umpire shall replace the Bowl.
(e) Displacement by dead Bowl – if a 'toucher' in the ditch be displaced by a dead Bowl from the rink of play, it shall be restored to its original position by a player of the opposite team or by the Marker.

39. 'Line Bowls'
A Bowl shall not be accounted as outside the line unless it be entirely clear of it. This shall be ascertained by looking perpendicularly down upon the Bowl or by placing a square on the green.

MOVEMENT OF JACK

40. A 'live' Jack in the Ditch
A Jack moved by a Bowl in play into the front ditch within the boundaries of the rink shall be deemed to be 'live'. It may be moved by the impact of a 'toucher' in play and also by the impact of a 'non-toucher' which remains in play after the impact, any movement of the Jack by such incidents

LAWS OF THE GAME

shall be valid. However, should the 'non-toucher' enter the ditch after impact, it shall be 'dead' and the Jack shall be deemed to have been 'displaced' by a 'dead' Bowl and the provisions of Law 48 shall apply. If the Jack in the ditch cannot be seen from the mat its position shall be marked by a white peg about 2 inches (51mm broad and not more than 4 inches (102mm) in height, placed upright on top of the bank immediately in line from the place where the Jack rests.

41. A Jack accounted 'dead'
Should the Jack be driven by a Bowl in play and come to rest wholly beyond the boundary of the rink, i.e. over the bank, or over the side boundary, or into any opening or inequality of any kind in the bank, or rebound to a distance of less than 61 feet (18.59 metres) in direct line from the centre of the front edge of the mat to the Jack in its rebounded position, it shall be accounted 'dead'.

(National Authorities have the option to vary the distance to which a Jack may rebound and still be playable for games other than International and Commonwealth Games.)

42. 'Dead' End
When the Jack is 'dead' the end shall be regarded as a 'dead' end and shall not be accounted as a played end even though all the Bowls in that end have been played. All 'dead' ends shall be played anew in the same direction unless both Skips or Opponents in Singles agree to play in the opposite direction. After a 'dead' end situation the right to deliver the Jack shall always return to the player who delivered the original Jack.

43. Playing to a boundary Jack
The Jack, if driven to the side boundary of the rink and not wholly beyond its limits, may be played to on either hand and, if necessary a Bowl may pass outside the side limits of the rink. A Bowl so played, which comes to rest within the boundaries of the rink, shall not be accounted 'dead'. If the Jack be driven to the side boundary line and comes rest partly within the limits of the rink, a Bowl played outside the limits of the rink and coming to rest entirely outside the boundary line, even though it has made contract with the Jack, shall be accounted 'dead' and shall be removed to the bank by a member of the player's team.

44. A Damaged Jack

The jack can be delivered to any length beyond the stipulated minimum, but it must always be central.

In the event of a Jack being damaged, the Umpire shall decide if another Jack is necessary and, if so, the end shall be regarded as a 'dead' end and another Jack shall be substituted and the end shall be replaced anew.

45. A Rebounding Jack
If the Jack is driven against the face of the bank and rebounds on to the rink, or after being played into the ditch, it be operated on by a 'toucher', so as to find its way on to the rink, it shall be played to in the same manner as if it had never left the rink.

46. Jack displacement
(a) By a player
If the Jack be diverted from its course while in motion on the green, or displaced while at rest on the green, or in the ditch, by any one of the players, the opposing Skip shall

have the Jack restored to its former position, or allow it to remain where it rests and play the end to a finish, or declare the end 'dead'.
(b) Inadvertently produced
If the Jack be moved at the time of measuring by a player it shall be restored to its former position by an opponent.

47. Jack Displaced by non-player
(a) If the Jack, whether in motion or at rest on the rink, or in the ditch, be displaced by a Bowl from another rink, or by any object or by an individual not a member of the team, the two Skips shall decide as to its original position, and if they unable to agree, the end shall be declared 'dead'.
(b) If a Jack be displaced by a Marker or Umpire it shall be restored by him to its original position of which he shall be the sole judge.

48. Jack displaced by 'non-toucher'
A Jack displaced in the rink of play by a 'non-toucher' rebounding from the bank shall be restored, or as near as possible, to its original position by a player of the opposing team. Should a Jack, however, after having been played into the ditch, be displaced by a 'dead' Bowl it shall be restored to its marked position by a player of the opposing side or by the Marker.

FOURS PLAY

The basis of the Game of Bowls is Fours Play

49. The rink and fours play
a) Designation of players. A team shall consist of four players, named respectively Lead, Second, Third and Skip, according to the order in which they play, each playing two Bowls.
(b) Order of Play. The Leads shall play their two Bowls alternately, and so on, each pair of players in succession to the end. No one shall play until his opponent's Bowl shall have come to rest. Except under circumstances provided for in Law 63, the order of play shall not be changed after the first end has been played, under penalty of disqualification, such penalty involving the forfeiture of the match or game to the opposing team.

50. Possession of the Rink.
Possession of the rink shall belong to the team whose Bowl is being played. The players in possession of the rink for the time being shall not be interfered with, annoyed, or have their attention distracted in any way by their opponents.
As soon as each Bowl shall have come to rest, possession of the rink shall be transferred to the other team, time being allowed for marking a 'toucher'.

51. Position of Players
Players of each team not in the act of playing or controlling play shall stand behind the Jack and away from the head, or 3 feet (92cm) behind the mat. As soon as the Bowl is delivered, the Skip or player directing, if in front of the Jack, shall retire behind it.

52. Players and their duties
(a) The Skip shall have sole charge of his team, and his instructions shall be observed by his players.
With the opposing Skip he shall decide all disputed points, and when both agree their decision shall be final. If both Skips cannot agree, the point in dispute shall be referred to, and considered by, an Umpire whose decision shall be final. A Skip may at any time delegate his powers and any of his duties to other members of his team provided that such delegation is notified to the opposing Skip.
(b) The Third. The third player may have deputed to him the duty of measuring any and all disputed shots.
(c) The Second. The second player shall keep a record of all shots scored for and against his team and shall at all times retain possession of the score card whilst play is in progress. He shall see that the names of all players are entered on the score card; shall compare his record of the game with that of the opposing second player as each end is declared, and at the close of the game shall hand his score card to his Skip.
(d) The Lead. The Lead shall place the mat, and shall deliver the Jack ensuring that the Jack is properly centred before playing his first Bowl.
(e) In addition to the duties specified in the preceding clauses, any player may undertake such duties as may be assigned to him by the Skip in Clause 52(a) hereof.

RESULT OF END

53. The Shot
A shot or shots shall be adjudged by the Bowl or Bowls nearer to the Jack than any Bowl played by the opposing player or players. When the last Bowl has come to rest, 30 seconds shall elapse, if either team desires, before the shots are counted.
Neither Jack nor Bowls shall be moved until each Skip has agreed to the number of shots, except in circumstances where a Bowl has to be moved to allow the measuring of another Bowl.

54. Measuring conditions to be observed.
No measuring shall be allowed until the end has been completed. All measurements shall be made to the nearest point of each object. If a Bowl requiring to be measured is resting on another Bowl which prevents its measurement, the best available means shall be taken to secure its position, whereupon the other Bowl shall be removed. The same course shall be followed where more than two Bowls are involved, or where, in the course of measuring, a single Bowl is in danger of falling or otherwise changing its position.

When it is necessary to measure to a Bowl or Jack in the ditch, and another Bowl or Jack on the green, the measurement shall be made with the ordinary flexible measure. Calipers may be used to determine the shot only when the Bowls in question and the Jack are on the same plane.

55. Tie – No shot

When at the conclusion of play in any end the nearest Bowl of each team is touching the Jack, or is deemed to be equidistant from the Jack, there shall be no score recorded. The end shall be declared drawn and shall be counted a played end.

56. Nothing in these Laws shall be deemed to make it mandatory for the last player to play his last Bowl in any end, but he shall declare to his opponent or opposing Skip his intention to refrain from playing it before the commencement of determining the result of the end and this declaration shall be irrevocable.

Game decisions

57. In the case of a single game or a team game or a side game played on one occasion, or at any stage of an eliminating competition, the victory decision shall be awarded to the player, team, or side of players producing at the end of the game, the higher total score of shots, or in the case of a 'game of winning ends' a majority of winning ends.

58. Tournament games and games in series

In the case of Tournament games or games in series, the victory decision shall be awarded to the player, team or side of players producing at the end of the tournament or series of contests, either the largest number of winning games or the highest net score of shots in accordance with the regulations governing the tournament or series of games.

Points may be used to indicate game successes.

Where points are equal, the aggregate shots scored against each team (or side) shall be divided into the aggregate shots it has scored. The team (or side) with the highest result shall be declared the winner.

59. Playing to a finish and possible drawn games

If in an eliminating competition, consisting of a stated or agreed upon number of ends, it be found, when all the ends have been played, that the scores are equal, an extra end or ends shall be played until a decision has been reached.

The Captains or Skips shall toss and the winner shall have the right to decide who shall play first. The extra end shall be played from where the previous end was completed, and the mat shall be placed in accordance with Law 24.

DEFAULTS OF PLAYERS IN FOURS PLAY

60. Absentee players in any team or side

(a) In a single Fours game, for a trophy, prize or other competitive award, where a club is represented by only one Four, each member of such Four shall be a bona fide member of the club. Unless all four players appear and are ready to play at the end of the maximum waiting period of 30 minutes, or should they introduce an ineligible player, then that team shall forfeit the match to the opposing team.
(b) In a domestic Fours game. Where, in a domestic Fours game the number of players cannot be accommodated in full teams of four players, three players may play against three players, but shall suffer the deduction of one-fourth of the total score of each team. A smaller number of players than six shall be excluded from that game.
(c) In a Side game. If within a period of 30 minutes from the time fixed for the game, a single player is absent from one or both teams in a side game, whether a friendly club match or a match for a trophy, prize or other award, the game shall proceed, but in the defaulting team, the number of Bowls shall be made up by the Lead and Second players playing three Bowls each, but one-fourth of the total shots scored by each four playing three men shall be deducted from their score at the end of the game.

Fractions shall be taken into account.
(d) In a Side game. Should such default take place where more Fours than one are concerned, or where a Four has been disqualified for some other infringement, and where the average score is to decide the contest, the scores of the non-defaulting Fours only shall be counted, but such average shall, as a penalty in the case of the defaulting side, be arrived at by dividing the aggregate score of that side by the number of Fours that should have been played and not as in the case of the other side, by the number actually engaged in the game.

61. Play irregularities

(a) Playing out of turn. When a player has played before his turn, the opposing Skip shall have the right to stop the Bowl in its course and it shall be played in its proper turn, but in the event of the Bowl so played, having moved or displaced the Jack or Bowl, the opposing Skip shall have the option of allowing the end to remain as it is after the Bowl so played has come to rest, or having the end declared 'dead'.
(b) Playing the wrong Bowl. A Bowl played by mistake shall be replaced by the player's own Bowl.
(c) Changing Bowls. A player shall not be allowed to change his Bowls during the course of a game, or in a resumed game, unless they be objected to, as provided in Law 9(d), or when a Bowl has been so damaged in the course of play as, in the opinion of the Umpire, to render the Bowl (or Bowls) unfit for play.
(d) Omitting to play
  (i) If the result of an end has been agreed upon, or the head has been touched in the agreed process of determining the result, then a player who forfeits or has omitted to play a Bowl, shall forfeit the right to play it.
  (ii) A player who has neglected to play a Bowl in the proper sequence shall forfeit the right to play such Bowl,

BOWL TO WIN

if a Bowl has been played by each team before such mistake was discovered.

(iii) If before the mistake be noticed, a Bowl has been delivered in the reversed order and the head has not been disturbed, the opponent shall then play two successive Bowls to restore the correct sequence.

If the head has been disturbed, clause 61(a) shall apply.

62. Play Interruptions

(a) Game Stoppages. When a game of any kind is stopped, either by mutual arrangement or by the Umpire, after appeal to him on account of darkness or the conditions of the weather, or any other valid reason, it shall be resumed with the scores as they were when the game stopped. An end commenced, but not completed, shall be declared null.
(b) Substitutes in a resumed game. If in a resumed game any one of the four original players be not available, one substitute shall be permitted as stated in Law 63 below. Players, however, shall not be transferred from one team to another.

INFLUENCES AFFECTING PLAY

63. Leaving the Green
If during the course of a side Fours, Triples or Pairs game a player has to leave the green owing to illness, or other reasonable cause, his place shall be filled by a substitute, if in the opinion of both Skips (or failing agreement by them, then in the opinion of the Controlling Body) such substitution is necessary. Should the player affected be a Skip, his duties and position in a Fours game shall be assumed by the Third player, and the substitute shall play either as a Lead, Second or Third. In the case of triples the substitute may play either as Lead or Second, but not as Skip and in the case of Pairs the substitute shall play as Lead only. Such substitute shall be a member of the club to which the team belongs. In domestic play National Authorities may decide the position of any substitute.

If during the course of a single-handed game, a player has to leave the green owing to illness, or reasonable cause, the provision of Law 62(a) shall be observed.

No player shall be allowed to delay the play by leaving the rink or team, unless with the consent of his opponent, and then only for a period not exceeding 10 minutes.

Contravention of this Law shall entitle the opponent or opposing team to claim the game or match.

64. Objects on the Green
Under no circumstances, other than as provided in Laws 29, 33 and 40, shall any extraneous object to assist a player be placed on the green, or on the bank, or on the Jack, or on a Bowl or elsewhere.

65. Unforeseen incidents
If, during the course of play, the position of the Jack or Bowls be disturbed by wind, storm, or by any neutral object the end shall be declared 'dead', unless the Skips are agreed as to the replacement of Jack or Bowls.

DOMESTIC ARRANGEMENTS

66. In addition to any matters specifically mentioned in these Laws, National Authorities may, in circumstances dictated by climate or other local conditions, make such other regulations as are deemed necessary and desirable, but such regulations must be submitted to the WBB for approval. For this purpose the Board shall appoint a Committee to be known as the Laws Committee with powers to grant approval or otherwise to any proposal, such decision being valid until the proposal is submitted to the Board for a final decision.

67. Local Arrangements
Constituent clubs of National Authorities shall also in making their domestic arrangements make such regulations as are deemed necessary to govern their club competitions, but such regulations shall comply with the Laws of the Game, and be approved by the Council of their National Authority.

68. National Visiting Teams or Sides
No team or side of Bowlers visiting overseas or the British Isles shall be recognized by the International Bowling Board unless it first be sanctioned and recommended by the National Authority to which its members are affiliated.

69. Contracting out
No club or club management committee or any individual shall have the right or power to contract out of any of the Laws of the Game as laid down by the World Bowls Board.

REGULATING SINGLE-HANDED, PAIRS AND TRIPLES GAMES

70. The foregoing laws, where applicable, shall also apply to Single-handed, Pairs and Triples games.

SPECTATORS

71. Persons not engaged in the game shall be situated clear of and beyond the limits of the rink of play, and clear of the verges. They shall neither by word nor act disturb or advise the players. This shall not apply to advice given by a Manager or in his absence his delegated deputy of a team or side.

Betting or gambling in connection with any game or games shall not be permitted or engaged in within the grounds of any constituent club.

LAWS OF THE GAME

DUTIES OF MARKER

72. (a) In the absence of the Umpire, the Marker shall control the game in accordance with the WBB Basic Laws. He shall, before play commences, examine all Bowls for the imprint of the IBB/WBB Stamp, or that of its National Authority, such imprint to be clearly visible, and shall ascertain by measurement the width of the rink of play (see note after Law 73).
(b) He shall centre the Jack, and shall place a full-length Jack 6 feet (1.84 metres) from the ditch.
(c) He shall ensure that the Jack is not less than 70 feet (21.35 metres) from the front edge of the mat, after it has been centred.
(d) He shall stand at one side of the rink, and to the rear of the Jack.
(e) He shall answer affirmatively or negatively a player's inquiry as to whether a Bowl is jack high. If requested, he shall indicate the distance of any Bowl from the Jack, or from any other Bowl, and also, if requested, indicate which Bowl he thinks is shot and/or the relative position of any other Bowl.
f) Subject to contrary directions from either opponent under Law 34 he shall mark all 'touchers' immediately they come to rest, and remove chalk marks from 'non-touchers'. With the agreement of both opponents he shall remove all dead Bowls from the green and the ditch. He shall mark the positions of the jack and touchers which are in the ditch. (See Laws 33 and 40.)
(g) He shall not move, or cause to be moved, either Jack or Bowls until each player has agreed to the number of shots.
(h) He shall measure carefully all doubtful shots when requested by either player. If unable to come to a decision satisfactory to the players, he shall call in an Umpire. If an official Umpire has not been appointed, the Marker shall select one. The decision of the Umpire shall be final.
(i) He shall enter the score at each end, and shall intimate to the players the state of the game. When the game is finished, he shall see that the score card, containing the names of the players, is signed by the players, and disposed of in accordance with the rules of the competition.

DUTIES OF UMPIRE

73. An Umpire shall be appointed by the Controlling Body of the Association, Club or Tournament Management Committee. His duties shall be as follows:
(a) He shall examine all Bowls for the imprint of the IBB/WBB Stamp, or that of its National Authority, and ascertain by measurement the width of the rinks of play.
(b) He shall measure any shot or shots in dispute, and for this purpose shall use a suitable measure. His decision shall be final.
(c) He shall decide all questions as to the distance of the mat from the ditch, and the Jack from the mat.
(d) He shall decide as to whether or not Jack and/or Bowls are in play.
(e) He shall enforce the Laws of the Game.
(f) In World Bowls Championships and Commonwealth Games, the Umpire's decision shall be final in respect of any breach of a Law, except that, upon questions relating to the meaning or interpretation of any Law, there shall be a right of appeal to the Controlling Body.

Measuring shots is one of the key duties of the umpire, and of course his decision is final.

INDEX

Across the Head 154
Aiming Point 154
Allcock, Tony 17, 20, 23, 33, 36, 40, 47, 51, 65, 77, 80, 104, 107, 114, 116, 117, 118, 120, 121, 124, 141
Arc 13, 16, 43, 44, 45

Backswing 31, 33, 36, 38, 49, 50, 51, 67
Backhand 53, 85, 88, 89, 90, 91, 92, 93, 94, 95, 100, 101, 102, 103, 105, 106, 136, 140
Bank 46, 92, 154
Bell, John 155
Bellis, Peter 34, 35, 110
Bias 12, 13, 14, 15, 36, 39, 43, 44, 54, 57, 62, 64, 65, 67, 72, 90, 98
Blocker/Block Shot 55, 67, 92, 98, 105, 114, 154
Bowls:
Back bowl 154
Composition 9, 13, 14
Lignum 9, 41
Bryant, Ann 20
Bryant, David 14, 16, 24, 29, 31, 33, 36, 38, 46, 50, 77, 80, 108, 115, 116, 117, 118, 119, 121, 139, 140

Cast 77
Centreline 44, 48, 76, 88, 92
Clevedon Club 139
Corkhill, David 84
Corsie, Richard 34
Count 154
County Championships 20

Dead Bowl 155
Dead End 155
Delivery 8, 24, 26, 36, 38, 39, 46, 48, 50, 51, 53, 64
Ditch 88, 91, 100, 104, 105, 106
Doubles 110
Draw Shot 52, 53, 57, 67, 70, 77, 89, 90, 91, 94, 95, 96, 99, 101, 102, 103, 104, 105, 114, 119, 120, 124, 136
Drive 14, 46, 55, 56, 57, 66, 67
Duff, Hugh 28

End 68, 76, 77, 84, 87, 98, 99
English Bowling Association 111
English National Association of Visually Handicapped Bowlers 20

Firm Wood 64, 65, 114, 120
Firing Shot 137
Follow Through 31, 41, 49, 50
Foot Fault 80
Footwear 18
Forward Swing 33, 36

Forehand 53, 85, 88, 90, 91, 92, 93, 94, 95, 97, 98, 100, 101, 102, 104, 105, 140
Fours 111, 122-132
Full House 106

Green 9, 13, 48, 59, 67, 83, 84, 85, 86, 93, 104
Artificial 81, 83
Fast 15, 38, 45, 48, 57
Indoor 81
Heavy 44, 59, 65, 71
Maintenance 75
Slow 59
Soggy 23

Greenspeed 70, 71
Uneven 41
Grips 8, 14
Claw 22, 24, 25, 36, 38, 39, 49, 77
Cradle 22, 41, 49, 77
Finger 24, 25

Head 68, 84, 85, 88, 90, 91, 100, 103, 107, 114, 119, 124, 125, 126, 127, 129, 139

Jack 20, 43, 44, 45, 47, 48, 49, 50, 51, 52, 53, 55, 60, 61, 62, 64, 66, 67, 70, 75, 76, 77, 78, 80, 83, 86, 87, 89, 91, 93, 94, 95, 96, 97, 98, 100, 101, 102, 103, 104, 105, 106, 107, 108, 114, 124, 131
High 92, 107, 109, 114
Johnston, Margaret 33
Johnson, Brian 61
Kingdon, Bryan 61

Lead 124, 125, 131
Length 42, 43, 44, 46, 48, 50, 51, 52, 53, 55, 67, 114, 115, 131, 139
Line 24, 36, 39, 41, 42, 43, 44, 45, 46, 47, 48, 51, 52, 53, 55, 57, 59, 67, 114, 139

Mat 31, 38, 41, 44, 45, 46, 49, 53, 70, 75, 76, 78, 80, 93, 94, 107, 125, 129, 131, 137
McClure, Ian 135
McQueen, Willie 58
Moseley, Bill 32

Number 2 124, 125, 126, 127, 131, 133
Number 3 126, 128, 129, 130, 131, 132, 133

Oliver, Ken 17
Ottaway, John 124, 125
Ovett, Oliver 18

Pairs (Rules) 111, 116, 121, 131
Parrella, Rob 30, 48, 66, 67

Percentage Shot 84, 85, 86, 90, 91, 94, 98, 103, 109, 139
Plant Shot 62, 63
Positional Draw 54, 55
Price, John 116

Rees, Stephen 116
Rest shot 56, 57, 58, 128, 156
Rink 44, 45, 46, 47, 48, 52, 66, 71, 75, 76, 91, 93, 98, 103, 107, 116, 128, 142

Schuback, Ian 107, 112
Serge, Dr Julius 32
Shot Selection 84
Shoulder of the Arc 43, 44, 45, 46, 47, 67
Singles 77, 110, 111, 112, 113, 114, 115, 125, 127, 128, 133
Skirts 21
Skips 57, 77, 78, 112, 116, 117, 118, 119, 120, 124, 126, 127, 128, 129, 130, 131, 132
Springing the Jack 157
Stance 8, 26, 36, 39, 46, 47, 48, 49, 50
Athletic 28, 30, 32, 33, 36, 38, 41, 46, 49
Crouch 29, 36, 39, 46, 50
Fixed 31, 32, 36
Semi Crouch/Low Athletic 30, 33, 38, 41, 49
South African Clinic/Semi-Fixed 32, 34

Tactics 68, 109, 132
Takeout Shot 86
Tap and Lie 58, 59, 89, 94, 99
Target Bowl 98
Taylor, Ian 35
Televised Tournaments 10, 21
Thomson, Andy 143
Tied End 157
Timing Shot 56, 64
Toucher 155
Tracking 75, 125
Trail Shot 60, 61, 97, 104, 105
Trial End 77, 108
Triples 111, 133

Weight 157
Wick Shot 62, 63, 95
Wilshire, Spencer 61
Wood, Willie 19, 28, 108
World Bowls Board 13, 111
World Championships (1988) 16, 17, 108
World Championships (Indoor) 16, 17, 82, 107
Pairs 117, 118, 120
Singles 112, 119, 143

Yard on Shot 56, 57, 58, 63, 67